A HINDU PERSPECTIVE ON THE PHILOSOPHY OF RELIGION

A Hindu Perspective on the Philosophy of Religion

ARVIND SHARMA

Associate Professor,
Faculty of Religious Studies,
McGill University, Montreal

St. Martin's Press New York

Scholarly and Reference Division,
St. Martin's Press, Inc., 175 Fifth Avenue, New York, N.Y. 10010

First Published in the United States of America in 1991

Printed in Great Britain

ISBN 0–312–05303–7

Library of Congress Cataloging-in-Publication Data
Sharma, Arvind.
A Hindu perspective on the philosophy of religion/Arvind Sharma.
p. cm.
Includes bibliographical references and index.
ISBN 0–312–05303–7
1. Religion—Philosophy. 2. Philosophy. Hindu. I. Title.
BL51.S49 1991
200'1—dc20

90–43340
CIP

For
Langdon Gilkey

Contents

Acknowledgements viii

Introduction ix

1 Grounds for Belief in God 1

2 Grounds for Disbelief in God 32

3 Hindu Theodicies: The Problem of Evil 46

4 Christian Views of Revelation in a Hindu Context 62

5 Religious Language 78

6 The Problem of Falsification and Verification 91

7 Human Destiny: Immortality and Resurrection 124

8 Karma and Reincarnation 140

9 The Truth-Claims of Different Religions 152

Glossary 166

For Further Reading 171

Index 172

Acknowledgements

Assistance received in the preparation of this book from the Faculty of Religious Studies, McGill University, Montreal, Canada; the Department of Religion, Temple University, Philadelphia, USA, and from the Department of Religious Studies, The University of Sydney, Sydney, Australia, is gratefully acknowledged.

Permission to use material in the first chapter, which first appeared in *The Scottish Journal of Religious Studies* 5 (2) pp. 134–40, is also gratefully acknowledged.

Introduction

It is customary to end prefatory notes such as this with an anecdote. I would like to start with one. As a graduate student I once had the audacity, arising doubtless out of lack of acquaintance, to ask Wilfred Cantwell Smith, as he left the hall after delivering his lecture: 'What is the difference between religion and philosophy?' Professor Smith arrested his forward motion when he heard the question, looked me over, and asked: 'Are you from India?' 'Yes', I said, complying simultaneously with the requirements of honesty and courtesy. 'In that case', he said, resuming his stride, 'for you there is no difference. For us, our philosophy comes from Greece and our religion comes from Palestine.'

The end of that conversation was the beginning of this book. This is not a book on Hindu philosophy nor is it a book on the Hindu religious tradition; nor a book on the philosophy of religion. Neither is it a book on Hindu philosophy of religion or a philosophy of the Hindu religion. It is something much more modest. It only claims to present to a student of the philosophy of religion something from the Hindu philosophical Weltanschauungen, which he, in his more cross-cultural and cosmopolitan moments, may contemplate with tolerant interest.

1

Grounds for Belief in God

I

The attitude towards the existence of God varies within the Hindu religious tradition.[1] This may not be entirely unexpected given the tolerance for doctrinal diversity for which the tradition is known. Thus of the six orthodox systems of Hindu philosophy only three address the question in some detail. These are the schools of thought known as Nyāya, Yoga and the theistic forms of Vedānta. Among these however the theistic forms of Vedānta assert the existence of God primarily on the basis of scriptural authority[2] so that from a philosophical point of view it is the proofs for the existence of God as adduced in Nyāya and Yoga which assume primary importance.

II

In considering the proofs of the existence of God in the Nyāya school of Hindu philosophy, a few fundamental facts must be kept in mind. Whereas in the Judeo-Christian tradition God is the creator of the universe and creates it *ex nihilo*, this is not the case with most of Hinduism. In much of Hinduism, and certainly in Nyāya, God is the efficient but not the material cause of the universe;[3] where, then, it might be asked, does this pre-existent matter come from? The answer is that it is eternal, like God.

The argument runs as follows. Any material element which is not capable of division constitutes an ultimate. Thus those constituents of matter which are infinitesimally small, for example atoms, or those which are infinitely large, for example space, are ultimates. It is out of these that God fashions the universe at the beginning of each aeon so that the various souls may obtain their just deserts according to their *karma*. This Hindu concept of karma, like that of pre-existing matter, also complicates the question of theistic proofs in Hinduism. It implies that God does not dispense justice directly but only indirectly, if at all, through *karma*.[4] Moral order is thus seen as built into the structure of the universe. In other words cosmological, teleological and moral arguments for the existence of God are indeed adduced in Hinduism as in Christianity but the theological matrices in which they appear are different.

Perhaps it is best to begin by recapitulating the role of God before examining the arguments for his existence. The basic text of the Nyāya school is the Nyāyasūtra, which pre-dates the Christian era. It contains three aphorisms involving God (IV.I.19–21), and from these the following points may be drawn: (a) that God is the efficient cause of the world; (b) that for dispensing man's fruits of action he is dependent on man's action; and (c) that this dependence of his does not in any way interfere with his sovereignty, inasmuch as man can neither work nor reap the fruits of his work but by and through the divine will.[5]

This, very briefly, is the role of God. But how do we know that someone who plays such a role exists?

The person best known in Hindu thought for providing the proofs for the existence of God is Udayana,[6] a scholar of the tenth century AD. He adduces these proofs in a work entitled the Nyāyakusumāñjali.[7] This book is widely regarded as a classic of Hindu theism and Udayana's proofs for the existence of God are as celebrated within Hinduism as Thomas Aquinas's are within Christianity. We now turn to an examination of these proofs.

III

The proofs of the existence of God provided by Udayana are presented tersely in aphorism V.1. They are nine in number and are summarised below for convenience:

(1) The world is an effect and hence it must have an efficient cause. This intelligent agent is God. The order, design, co-ordination between different phenomena come from God. (*kāryāt*)

(2) The atoms being essentially inactive cannot form the different combinations unless God gives motion to them. The Unseen Power, the Adṛṣṭa, requires the intelligence of God.

Without God it cannot supply motion to the atoms. (*āyojanāt*)

(3) The world is sustained by God's will. Unintelligent Adṛṣṭa cannot do this. And the world is destroyed by God's will. (*dhṛtyādeḥ*)

(4) A word has a meaning and signifies an object. The power of words to signify their objects comes from God. (*padāt*)

(5) God is the author of the infallible Veda. (*pratyayataḥ*)

(6) The Veda testifies to the existence of God. (*shruteḥ*)

(7) The Vedic sentences deal with moral injunctions and prohibitions. The Vedic commands are the Divine commands. God is the creator and promulgator of the moral laws. (*vākyāt*)

(8) According to Nyāya-Vaisheṣika the magnitude of a dyad is not produced by the infinitesimal magnitude of the two atoms each, but by the *number* of the two atoms. Number 'one' is directly perceived, but other numbers are conceptual creations. Numerical conception is related to the mind of the perceiver. At the time of creation, the souls are unconscious. And the atoms and the Unseen Power and space, time, minds are all unconscious. Hence the numerical conception depends upon the Divine Consciousness. So God must exist. (*saṅkhyāvisheṣāt*)

(9) We reap the fruits of our own actions. Merit and demerit accrue from our actions and the stock of merit and demerit is called Adṛṣṭa, the Unseen Power. But this Unseen Power, being unintelligent, needs the guidance of a supremely intelligent God. (*adṛṣṭāt*)[8]

The reader will notice that except for the first three the proofs are so specific to Hinduism as to involve a rather elaborate explication particular to Hinduism if they are to be included in the discussion. It will be best therefore to concentrate our attention on the first three, especially as they parallel the traditional proofs of the existence of God adduced in Western philosophy.[9] In this case the best convergence is provided by the five arguments associated with Thomas Aquinas (1224/5–1274).

> Aquinas's proofs start from some general feature of the world around us and argue that there could not be a world with this particular characteristic unless there were also the ultimate reality which we call God. The first Way argues from the fact of

> motion to a Prime Mover; the second from causation to a First Cause; the third from contingent beings to a Necessary Being; the fourth from degrees of value to Absolute Value; and the fifth from evidences of purposiveness in nature to a Divine Designer.[10]

A little comparative reflection suggests that there is a clear correspondence between at least four proofs of the existence of God advanced by Aquinas's and Udayana's proofs though Udayana's second proof needs to be broken up into (2a) and (2b) to achieve numerical correspondence.

AQUINAS	UDAYANA
Prime Mover	(2a)
First Cause	(1)
Necessary Being	(3)
Absolute Value	—
Divine Design	(2b)

Let us concentrate now on the argument by design, which is included in the first argument of Udayana and constitutes the last of Aquinas's. This teleological argument has an extremely interesting background in the context of Indian thought. The crux of the matter of course is whether the existence of design necessarily implies a conscious intelligent designer. This point is raised by David Hume (1711–1776)[11] in his critique of the teleological argument. For it can be argued that design could be natural to the universe. If the design is not regarded as natural, but as indicating the existence of an intelligence over and above the natural, then adequate grounds must be indicated for making such an inference.

The Indian critique of the teleological argument by design is interesting for it was argued by the Indian materialists, like their counterparts the scientific materialists of today, that Nature suffices by itself. There is no need to presume the existence of God just because the universe displays design, for such design could naturally inhere in it. This aspect of Indian materialism is known as *svabhāvavāda* of which indeed 'naturalism' will not be a bad translation. As such

> it traced whatever character an object might manifest to that very object and not to any extraneous agent. It accordingly rejected

the idea that nature reveals any divine or transcendental power working behind it. 'Fire is hot; water, cold; and the air is temperate to the touch. Who could have brought such distinctions into being, if they were not of the very essence (*svabhāva*) of those objects?' That is, things are what they are; and their nature, by itself, explains all the variety of the universe and the order that is noticeable in it.[12]

The other objection to the teleological argument comes from the school of Hindu thought known as Sāṅkhya. As this school developed a theistic version subsequently[13] it may be made clear that one is talking here of classical atheistic Sāṅkhya. In this system the existence of God is not admitted. There exists a plurality of souls who are called *puruṣas*. The system is thus fundamentally dualistic and sees the universe as composed of spirits and matter. Matter or *prakṛti* subserves the spirits. What is of interest here is the extent to which the teleological argument has been transferred to Nature from God. Indeed 'Sāṁkhya asserts that the teleology of the prakṛti is sufficient to explain all order and arrangement of the cosmos'.[14] According to it 'it is as easy to believe that the universe made itself as to believe that the maker of the universe made himself'.[15]

It should be noted that although both the Indian materialists and atheistic Sāṅkhya regard the teleological argument as not pointing to God, in the case of Sāṅkhya, spiritual beings called *puruṣas* are involved, but not God.

The Nyāya school tried to respond to these challenges. In fact it adduces some arguments which might have a bearing on the Western discussion of the subject as well. One of the arguments advanced against the teleological argument for God is that there is a difference between, for example a watch or a jug as effects, which are in fact artefacts and natural effects like mountains or oceans. Moreover it is argued that the universe may be more like a shoot sprouting from a seed, that is, a natural phenomenon rather than something artificially constructed like a watch. Nyāya meets the first point by saying that both jugs and rivers, so to speak, are effects and that

the concomitance between two things must be taken in its general aspect neglecting the specific peculiarities of each case of observed concomitance. Thus I had seen many cases of the

> concomitance of smoke with fire, and had thence formed the notion that 'wherever there is smoke there is fire'; but if I had only observed small puffs of smoke and small fires, could I say that only small quantities of smoke could lead us to the inference of fire, and could I hold that therefore large volumes of smoke from the burning of a forest should not be sufficient reason for us to infer the existence of fire in the forest?[16]
>
> As for the case of shoots sprouting the Nyāya
>
> answer is that even they are created by God, for they are also effects. That we do not see any one to fashion them is not because there is no maker of them, but because the creator cannot be seen. If the objector could distinctly prove that there was no invisible maker shaping these shoots, then only could he point to it as a case of contradiction. But so long as this is not done it is still only a doubtful case of enquiry and it is therefore legitimate for us to infer that since all effects have a cause, the shoots as well as the manifest world being effects must have a cause. This cause is Īśvara.[17]

It is clear that the whole issue is ultimately going to turn on the exact epistemological status of inference.

IV

The other school of Hindu thought which adduces proofs for the existence of God is Yoga.

> The proofs advanced for His existence are: (a) The Veda tells us that God exists; (b) the law of continuity tells us that there must be the highest limit of knowledge and perfection which is God; (c) God is responsible for the association and dissociation of Puruṣa and Prakṛti; (d) devotion to God is the surest way of obtaining concentration and thereby liberation.[18]

Out of these, again, proofs (a), (c) and (d) are particular to the school but (b) creates room for the incorporation of some further elements of Western proofs for the existence of God into the discussion.

Yogasūtras I.24–27 explain the nature of God (Īśvara) and some of them have been construed as providing proof for the existence of God. It is the purpose of this section to determine the type of argument for the existence of God – the ontological, the teleological and so on – to which they most closely correspond.

The concerned *sūtras* may first of all be briefly presented.

I.24: KLEŚAKARMAVIPĀKĀŚAYAḤ APARĀMṚṢṬAḤ PURUṢA-VIŚEṢA ĪŚVARAḤ
Untouched by hindrances or Karmas or fruition or by latent deposits the Īśvara is a special kind of self.

I.25: TATRA NIRATIŚAYAM SARVAJÑABĪJAM
In this [Īśvara] the germ of the omniscient is at the utmost excellence.

I.26: SA EṢA PŪRVEṢĀMAPI-GURUḤ KALENĀNAVACCHEDĀT
Teacher of the Primal (Sages) also, forasmuch as (with Him) there is no limitation by time.

I.27: TASYA VĀCAKAḤ PRAṆAVAḤ
The word-expressing Him is the mystic-syllable (*praṇava*).[19]

M. Hiriyanna treats *sūtra* I.25 as constituting an argument for the existence of God. After noting the difference between the concept of God in Yoga in relation to some other forms of Hinduism he remarks:

> The argument of his existence is that the gradation of knowledge, power and such other excellences which we notice in men necessarily suggests a Being who possesses those excellences in a superlative form. In thus interpreting the mere notion of a perfect Being as implying its actual existence, Patañjali is relying on what is known in Western philosophy as the ontological argument. It is that necessary Being which is called God. He is accordingly a perfect Puruṣa and has always been so. He embodies in himself all that is good and great, and the conception is personal. He is therefore unique; and even the liberated Puruṣas do not stand on the same footing, for he has never known, like them, the trammels of *saṁsāra*. On account of his perfection, he serves as a pattern to man in regard to what he might achieve. In this respect, he resembles a *guru* who ought, likewise, to be an

> embodiment of the ideal. It is devotion to God so conceived that is meant by the last of the ten commandments, and it signifies a complete surrender of oneself to him.[20]

Hiriyanna thus identifies *sūtra* I.25 as providing an ontological proof of the existence of God.

The ontological proof for the existence of God was first formulated by Anselm and the argument assumes two forms. The first form of the argument maintains that if God as

> the most perfect conceivable thing existed only in the mind, we should then have the contradiction that it is possible to conceive of a yet more perfect being, namely, the same being existing in reality as well as in the mind. Therefore, the most perfect conceivable being must exist in reality as well as in the mind.[21]

The second form of the argument maintains God's uniquely necessary existence.

> Since God as infinitely perfect is not limited in or by time, the twin possibilities of God's having ever come to exist or ever ceasing to exist are likewise excluded and God's non-existence is rendered impossible.[22]

Now to which of these two forms of the argument is Hiriyanna referring? Or is he referring to both?

It seems reasonably obvious that Hiriyanna is referring to the first form of the argument as he refers to 'the mere notion of a perfect Being as implying its actual existence', which was criticised by Gaunilo, a contemporary critic of Anselm, on precisely the ground that just because one can think of something perfect does not necessarily imply that it is real.

Further reflection on the *sūtra* suggests that in fact it is not suggestive of the first form of the ontological argument for the *sūtra* does not deal with the question of the distinction of existence of a perfect being in reality and in the mind. The argument does not rest on concept *per se* but rather on the conception of continuity.

> According to the law of continuity, whatever has degrees must have a lower and an upper limit. There are, for instance, different magnitudes, small and great. An atom is the smallest magni-

tude, while ākāśa or space is the greatest magnitude. Similarly, there are different degrees of knowledge and power. So there must be a person who possesses perfect knowledge and perfect power. Such a supreme person is God, the highest. There cannot be any self who is equal to God in power and knowledge, for in that case, there will be conflict and clash of desires and purposes between them, and a consequent chaos in the world.[23]

This line of argument is less in keeping with the first form of Anselm's ontological proof for the existence of God and more in keeping with the fourth way through which Thomas Aquinas tries to establish the existence of God 'from degrees of value to Absolute Value'.

It seems, then, that Hiriyanna incorrectly identifies *sūtra* I.25 as corresponding to the first form of Anselm's ontological proof of the existence of God.

A review of the *sūtras* cited at the beginning of the paper suggests, however, that in fact there is room for identifying elements of the *second* form of the ontological requirement, based on aseity, therein. For the *sūtra* I.26 describes Īśvara as free from the limitation of time (*kālena anavacchedāt*).

Aseity basically implies freedom from the limitation of time. It will now be demonstrated that in *sūtras* I.24 and I.26 such freedom is asserted in at least three ways, especially if the commentarial material is also taken into account. In order to appreciate the point however it is important to bear in mind the special nature of Īśvara as visualised within the philosophical system of Yoga.

Yoga, in line with Sāṅkhya, admits of a plurality of individual souls called *puruṣas*. These souls undergo suffering when in the trammels of *prakṛti* or matter but when they realise their own true nature they achieve salvation which is significantly called *kaivalya* or isolation, that is, from *prakṛti*. Even the term Yoga itself needs to be understood carefully on account of this feature of the system. Thus, though the term *Yoga* (derived from *yuj* to join) is cognate with the word 'yoke' and in several schools of thought, 'means the way to union with the ultimate reality' in 'the Sāṅkhya-Yoga however it stands for *vi-yoga* or separation – separation of the *puruṣa* from *prakṛti*'.[24]

Now when these *puruṣas* become liberated they also realise their own perfection like God. In relation to the realised *puruṣas* God is *primus inter pares*. Then what sets him apart from the rest?

In the context of the *sūtras* under consideration the following three constituencies of *puruṣas* need to be specially considered: (a) the *puruṣas* or souls who were *once* bound (*baddha*) but are now liberated; (b) the class of *puruṣas* called *prakṛtilayas* whose mind is resolved into primary matter and who are in a quasi-state of isolation; and (c) the ancient sages who proclaim the path of *yoga*. Now all of these groups represent *puruṣas* and it should be noted that Īśvara too is a *puruṣa*. Wherein then does his superiority over these three groups lie?

In all the cases his superiority has to do with time. In the case of the third group, that of the sages, he is their teacher 'not being limited by time'. He is the primordial teacher of Yoga. As for the first and second groups, as the famous commentator on the Yogasūtra called Vyāsa points out, although other *puruṣas* by cutting off their bonds in a sense are like God, yet God remains superior to them because he neither has fallen nor will fall into the trammels of *prakṛti*.

> Are all those, then, who have reached the state of absolute freedom Īśvaras, and there are many such for they have reached the state of absolute freedom after cutting the three bonds? No, Īśvara never had, or will have, any relation to these bonds. As former bondage is known in the case of the emancipated, not so in the case of Īśvara. Or, as future bondage is possible in the case of the *prakṛtilayas*, not so in the case of Īśvara. He is ever free, ever the Lord.[25]

The following conclusions may therefore be safely drawn on the basis of the above discussion: (a) that *sūtra* I.25 does not correspond to the first form of Anselm's ontological argument for the existence of God *pace* Hiriyanna (b) that *sūtras* I.24 and I.26 seem to correspond to the second form of Anselm's ontological argument for the existence of God (c) that *sūtra* I.25 seems to correspond to the fourth way adopted by Thomas Aquinas to demonstrate the existence of God.

V

In the preceding sections the proofs for the existence of God as found in the Nyāya and Yoga schools of Hindu philosophy were examined. We may now examine the discussion on this point as it is found in the theism of Rāmānuja. At this point we encounter a discontinuity. While Nyāya, and Yoga as well to a certain extent, try to establish the existence of God through reason, Rāmānuja rejects this approach and claims that the existence of God can be established by revelation alone.[26] We face the paradoxical situation in which someone trying to establish the existence of God does so by demonstrating the inadequacy of the rational grounds for belief in God on rational grounds. Three broad positions can be distinguished in this context. First there is the Nyāya position that

> revelation is valid, because it is the work of an omniscient author, and the existence of the latter can be established by inference. Thus the trustworthiness of scripture is not intrinsic, but is based upon the theistic proofs. Second, at the other extreme, Rāmānuja argues that the proofs are doubtful, because of the powerful objections which can be raised against them. Belief in God therefore rests solely upon revelation. Madhva, thirdly, represents an intermediate position – namely, that though the proofs themselves are doubtful if the truth of revelation is in question, they may become convincing if that truth is already conceded.[27]

We shall confine the discussion here to Rāmānuja. He offers a comprehensive critique of the various theistic proofs of the existence of God, specially of the teleological, the cosmological and the ontological.

One may begin by restating the 'explicitly teleological form' of the argument: 'it is because mountains, etc., have an analogy to artifacts in being wholes made of parts, that one can infer an intelligent agent'.[28] Rāmānuja produces the following counter-arguments, among others: (a) that natural features such as mountains cannot be compared to artefacts because, unlike artefacts, they 'can neither be produced, nor can their material and other causes be known; we therefore have no right to infer for them intelligent producers';[29] (b) that the argument by design is based on inference and that one would like to test the results of inference by sense-perception or experimentation which is not possible in this case;[30] (c) that even if we infer intelligent agency from the fact of design there might exist a multiplicity of such agencies (that is, specially evolved souls) rather than one God;[31] (d) 'Moreover, if you use the attribute of being an effect (which belongs to the totality of things) as a means to prove the existence of one omniscient and omnipotent creator, do you view this attribute as belonging to all things in so far as produced together, or in so far as produced in succession? In the former case the attribute of being an effect is not established (for experience does not show that all things are produced together); and in the latter case the attribute would really prove what is contrary to the hypothesis of one creator (for experience shows that things produced in succession have different causes). In attempting to prove the agency of one intelligent creative being only, we thus enter into conflict with Perception and Inference';[32] (e) 'Rāmānuja admits – or at least raises no objection to the view – that inference on the basis of finite agency need not necessarily establish that the creator of the material world suffers from all the limitations of a finite agent. Nevertheless, he contends, it cannot warrant our predicating of the creator perfections to which there is no analogy in what we know of finite agents.'[33]

The teleological argument is really discussed in two versions by Rāmānuja. One version – which may be called the material version – was discussed above. The spiritual version of the argument runs as follows: 'just as from the existence of a living body, we infer the existence of a soul or intelligent principle which animates it, so from the existence of non-sentient matter in the world, we may infer the existence of an Intelligent principle which animates and supports it'.[34] Rāmānuja rejects this spiritual version of the teleological argument based on analogical reasoning on the following grounds: (a) we wish to show God 'creates' the world, but the soul does not create the body; (b) we wish to show God *alone* supports the world, while the body is supported by relatives and so on, as well; (c) the fact that the body functions as a psychophysical organism does not by itself imply the existence of a soul; (d) living bodies breathe but earth, seas, mountains and so on, do not; (e) 'just as there are many souls animating many bodies' the inanimate material world could be traced to many intelligences and need not imply one God.[35] Thus whether on the analogy of a body presupposing an intelligent principle or of products presupposing a producing agent, the existence of God cannot be established.[36]

The cosmological argument was countered by Rāmānuja with the following comment:

> Is the cosmos supposed to have been produced all at one time, or in successive phases? The former supposition is unwarranted, since there is no evidence that the cosmos was created at one time. The second supposition would support the wrong conclusion – for experience shows that the effects produced at different times are produced by different agents.[37]

The ontological argument is not countered so much by Rāmānuja as by modern thinkers of his school. They point out that 'the concept of reality is different from the reality itself. It is absurd to prove the existence of God from the idea of God; existence can never be the predicate of a judgement and can only be the subject'.[38]

It is the suprasensible nature of Brahman, Rāmānuja insists, which puts it beyond the reach of rational proofs and confirms the conclusion that 'with regard to supersensuous matters, Scripture alone is authoritative, and that reasoning is to be applied only to the support of Scripture'.[39]

Here we come face to face with a basic difference in approach within Hindu theism on the relationship between God and revelation. According to the Nyāya school 'what is taught in the Veda is valid because its author, God, is all-knowing. It does not in this involve itself in a circle since it bases its belief in the existence of God not on revelation as the Vedānta does but on reason'.[40] On the other hand Rāmānuja, along with some other schools of Vedānta, takes the opposite stance: God exists because the Vedas say so and the Vedas are authoritative and self-valid.[41] This takes us into the next section.

VI

The modern mind is likely to baulk at the suggestion that such a weighty matter as the existence of God be decided by recourse to scriptural authority. It may satisfy a believer or an 'ordinary person'

> but a critical philosopher may say that scriptural testimony has no importance for philosophy, which is satisfied with nothing short of logically valid arguments in the attainment of true

> knowledge about anything, human or divine. So long as these are not forthcoming, the appeal to authority is of no avail.[42]

Modern Hindu thinkers have, therefore, examined the grounds for appealing to scriptural authority in such matters and have drawn some far-reaching conclusions. One of them is that while the traditional proofs of God may seem to provide a logical basis for belief in God, they can all be shown to be flawed in some way as some philosophers in the West such as Immanuel Kant and Hermann Lotze themselves recognise.[43] The basic problem is that to 'prove anything is to deduce it as a necessary conclusion from certain given premises. But God being the highest of all premises, the ultimate reality, there cannot be any anterior premise or premises from which we can deduce God as a conclusion.'[44] This is said to hold true, for instance, of the ontological, the cosmological and the teleological proofs. Thus:

> The ontological proof starts from the idea of the most perfect being and infers its existence on the ground that without existence it would not be most perfect. So, the cosmological argument starts from the sensible world as a finite and conditioned reality, and argues to the existence of an infinite, unconditioned and supersensible reality as the ground thereof. Similarly, the teleological proof lays stress on the adaptation of means to ends which we find so often in nature and infers the existence of an infinitely intelligent creator of the world. But all these proofs are vitiated by the fallacy of deducing the existence of God from the mere idea of Him. The idea of the most perfect being may involve the idea of existence, but not actual existence, just as the thought of one hundred rupees[45] in my pocket involves the image or the idea of their existence, but not their real physical existence. So, to think of the conditioned world we have to think of the unconditioned, or to explain the adaptation of things we have to think of an intelligent cause. But to think of the existence of something is not to prove its existence, since the *thought of existence* is not actual existence.[46]

It has thus been claimed that 'in truth mere reasoning or logical argument cannot prove the existence of anything'.[47] This seems like an overstatement but is really meant to draw attention to the fact that the existence of a thing is known through experience,[48] that there are some people who have experienced God,[49] that the scriptures are the embodiment of their knowledge[50] and may therefore 'be accepted as a source of right knowledge about God. Just as the great scientists and their sciences have been, for all ages, the source of our knowledge of many scientific truths', the Vedas 'constitute a just ground of our belief in one universal spiritual truth, God'.[51]

This argument, that God is known by direct experience and through the testimony of those by whom he has been experienced is not new, for Udayana says: 'By some he is also directly perceived.'[52] What is new is the emphasis placed on experience by both the absolutists and the theists within Hinduism. Hiriyanna concludes a discussion on the place of reason in absolutism or Advaita Vedānta with the remark: 'Thus we finally get beyond both reason and revelation, and rest on direct experience (*anubhava*) . . . Further, we should not forget that revelation itself, . . . goes back to the intuitive experience of the great seers of the past.'[53] And P. N. Srinivasachari, after discussing the inadequacy of the logical proofs of the existence of God as demonstrated by Rāmānuja remarks: 'Though the existence of God cannot be proved, He can be experienced by means of direct intuition.'[54]

It is against this background that the otherwise initially cryptic statement by S. Radhakrishnan seems to gain its full meaning:

> To say that God exists means that spiritual experience is attainable. The possibility of the experience constitutes the most conclusive proof of the reality of God. God is 'given', and is the factual content of the spiritual experience. All other proofs are descriptions of God, matters of definition, and language. The fact of God does not depend on mere human authority or evidence from alleged miraculous events. The authority of scripture, the traditions of the Church, or the casuistries of schoolmen who proclaim but do not prove, may not carry conviction to many of us who are the children of science and reason, but we must submit to the fact of spiritual experience, which is primary and positive. We may dispute theologies, but cannot deny facts. The fire of life in its visible burning compels assent, though not the fumbling speculations of smokers sitting around the fire.[55]

In the earlier comments the experiential bias of Hindu thought was highlighted. It is therefore not entirely surprising that the discussion of the grounds for belief in the existence of God has acquired an experiential dimension.

VII

The proof of God's existence as based on direct experience would fall under the category of 'The Argument from Special Events and Experiences' as discussed in the modern philosophy of religion.[56] These special events could be of two kinds: public and private.

Public events of this kind are usually regarded as miracles. In Hinduism however as distinguished from Christianity, such miracles need not necessarily be attributed to God, or be adduced as proof of his existence. They are explained in terms of psychic powers and these powers are *not* necessarily associated with theism. The following incident from the early days of Buddhism illustrates the point, as it is well known that Buddhism is not theistic in the usually accepted sense. The incident is connected with a monk who bore the name of Piṇḍola Bhāradvāja. A leading businessman of a capital city 'had placed a sandal-wood bowl on a high pole and challenged any holy person to bring it down. Piṇḍola heard of this . . . rose in the air by magic power and brought it down'.[57] When the Buddha heard of this he had the order of monks convened and questioned the venerable Piṇḍola Bhāradvāja saying:

> 'Is it true, as is said, Bhāradvāja, that the bowl of the (great) merchant of Rājagaha was fetched down by you?'
>
> 'It is true, Lord.' The Awakened one, the Lord rebuked him, saying:
>
> 'It is not suiting, Bhāradvāja, it is not becoming, it is not fitting, it is not worthy of a recluse, it is not allowable, it is not to be done. How can you, Bhāradvāja, on account of a wretched wooden bowl exhibit a condition of further-men, a wonder of psychic power to householders? As, Bhāradvāja, a woman exhibits her loin-cloth on account of a wretched stamped *māsaka*,[58] even so by you, Bhāradvāja, was a condition of further-men, a wonder of psychic power exhibited to householders on account of a wretched wooden bowl. It is not, Bhāradvāja, for pleasing

> those who are not (yet) pleased . . . .' Having rebuked him, having given reasoned talk, he addressed the monks, saying:
>
> 'Monks, a condition of further-men, a wonder of psychic power is not to be exhibited to householders. Whoever should exhibit them, there is an offence of wrong-doing. Break, monks, this wooden bowl; having reduced it to fragments, give them to monks as perfume to mix with ointment. And, monks, a wooden bowl should not be used. Whoever should use one, there is an offence of wrong-doing'.[59]

Christianity itself is in a sense based on a miracle, and the Gospel accounts mention several. The modern Hindu attitude on this point borders on the sceptical. When the modern Indian thinker Rammohun Roy published the New Testament he excluded some of those 'very special events and experiences' of a historical and miraculous nature which committed Christians find compelling. He justified his procedure in these terms:

> I feel persuaded that by separating from the other matters contained in the New Testament, the moral precepts found in that book, these will be more likely to produce the desirable effect of improving the hearts and minds of men of different persuasions and degrees of understanding. For, historical, and some other passages, are liable to the doubts and disputes of free thinkers and anti-christians, especially, miraculous relations, which are much less wonderful than the fabricated tales handed down to the natives of Asia, and consequently would be apt, at best, to carry little weight with them. On the contrary, moral doctrines, tending evidently to the maintenance of the peace and harmony of mankind at large, are beyond the reach of metaphysical perversion, and intelligible alike to the learned and to the unlearned. This simple code of religion and morality is so admirably calculated to elevate men's ideas to high and liberal notions of one GOD, who has equally subjected all living creatures, without distinction of cast[e], rank, or wealth, to change, disappointment, pain and death, and has equally admitted all to be partakers of the bountiful mercies which he has lavished over nature, and is also so well fitted to regulate the conduct of the human race in the discharge of their various duties to GOD, to themselves and to society, that I cannot but hope the best effects from its promulgation in the present form.[60]

The special private experience of God may now be considered. John H. Hick remarks that 'dramatic manifestations of God in vision and dream, by inner voice, numinous feeling, or mystical or ecstatic experience have also convinced many of the reality of God. Once again, though, it is not possible to found upon these experiences a general proof of divine existence'.[61]

Hindu thought investigates this point at some length. It takes mystical experience involving a claim of a direct access to reality seriously. For within Hindu thought, as shown earlier, 'it became fairly clear that arguments for God's existence could at best be a subsidiary means of persuasion as Madhva held. Of more importance perhaps was the assumption that religious experience gives an insight into the nature of ultimate reality',[62] that is, in this context, of God. In this context the Hindu thinker

> Kumārila raised a central problem: the experience of the individual may be delusory and so has to be checked by other evidence. Likewise, the Jainas argued that in so far as spiritual intuition is appealed to in establishing the existence of a Lord, it is as well to ask whether the belief in a Lord derives from the experience or conversely. Kumārila went on to affirm that the other evidence needed to check the intuition was provided by scripture, which is itself accepted by the general consensus.[63]

The interesting point here is that both Kumārila and the Jainas[64] were atheists, but Kumārila by implication also criticises them, though they both jointly criticise theism. This raises an interesting point about the validity of the persuasive force of an individual's experience, whether theistic or non-theistic.

> We may take as a good example of it Jainism, which traces its truths to the insight of great prophets like Mahāvīra . . . . In this appeal to the experience of an individual, others see a risk for, in their view, nobody's private insight can carry with it the guarantee of its own validity. As *Kumārila*, a well-known leader of orthodox thought, has remarked in discussing a related topic, a 'vision' that has unfolded itself to but one single person may after all be an illusion . . . . To avoid this possible defect of subjectivity orthodox thinkers postulate in the place of testimony, based upon the intuition of a single sage, another, viz. 'revelation'.[65]

The strictly traditional concept of revelation, that is, as the word of God or as eternal in itself is not of much of help here, but another point which has been developed in this context is suggestive. The fundamental criticism of the 'argument from special events and experiences' is that of subjectivity, the fact that the experience 'can be construed in other ways'. In this context the Hindu tradition may be seen as relying on a *plurality* of both the experiencers and the respondents to authenticate the experience. Hinduism has no *single* founder; its foundational scriptures, the Vedas, are based on the collective experience of the ancient sages. Within Hinduism the condition has also 'sometimes' been laid down as 'essential to all "revealed" teaching, viz. that is should have proved acceptable to the best minds (mahājana) of the community'.[66] Thus there is a double check against subjectivity if the revelation is viewed in purely human terms.[67]

VIII

Before this chapter is concluded it might be useful to pause awhile and consider such arguments in Hindu theism for the existence of God as might be analogous to the moral argument in the philosophy of religion. John H. Hick identifies two forms of the moral argument. The first form may be basically 'presented as a logical inference from objective moral laws to a divine Law Giver' and the second form basically argues that 'anyone seriously committed to respect moral values as exercising a sovereign claim upon his or her life must thereby implicitly believe in the reality of a trans-human source and the basis of these values which religion calls God'.[68]

The examination of the moral argument in the light of Hindu thought inevitably involves a consideration of the doctrine of karma. The first form of the argument can be seen as corresponding to the view that God has established and God supervises the operations of the 'law' of karma. Thus Śaiva theism maintained that (a) as the 'apportionment of good and evil in accordance with a person's deeds' required perfect knowledge of the moral law which God alone possessed, karma implied God; (b) karma by itself is inert and could only operate at the instigation of God and therefore again implied the existence of God.[69] Argument (b) is interesting in that it is also made by a twentieth century Indian

Śaiva mystic called Ramana Maharṣi who represents the absolutistic strand in Hindu thought more prominently than the theistic.[70] But as Ninian Smart notes: 'the notion that karma is self-operative is too deeply entrenched in Indian religious thought for such arguments to meet with much agreement'.[71]

The second form of the moral argument is also absorbed by the doctrine of karma and does not lead to the presumption of God's existence, for karma is itself involved in the question of moral values very deeply[72] and is a law which transcends the individuals; but it is not God.[73]

A further point needs to be made now and it is a delicate one. Hindu thought is much more prone to the consideration and even the judicious acceptance of pragmatic norms, norms which are not *solely* moral, while Western thought is committed to the 'supremacy of moral values'[74], perhaps even uncritically:

> We weep for Socrates, defender of reason, damned by the citizens of Athens on the trumped-up charge of corrupting the youth, but do not bother to investigate Nietzsche, damned without examination by the citizens of the modern world on the trumped-up charge of being responsible for Hitler.[75]

On the other hand,

> the ultimate value recognized by classical Hinduism in its most sophisticated sources is not morality but freedom, not rational self-control in the interests of the community's welfare but complete control over one's environment – something which includes self-control but also includes control over others and even control of the physical sources of power in the universe.[76]

Thus, inasmuch as Hindu thought might tend in the direction of power or take an antinomian transethical stance at certain points[77] the application of the moral argument is likely to be restricted, though it must be added that this is less likely to happen in the case of theism than absolutism.[78] But let us stay with theism and turn to the Śaiva form of it for further consideration.

In the schools of philosophy associated with Śaivism one also meets with other arguments for the existence of God.[79] But as Śiva is often regarded as the destroyer of the universe one gets an argument built around the destroyership rather than the creatorship of God! We have here a new twist to the cosmological argument. The argument by destruction – or what we might call the apocalyptic argument proceeds at two levels. At one level it is used to establish the existence of God; at another level it is used to establish the existence of Śiva as the supreme God over and above the rest. This second form of the argument is admittedly more sectarian in nature but makes an interesting philosophical point. Let us however first examine the argument at the first level.

It may be useful to begin by pointing out that, in Śaivism, God is treated as the performer of all the three cosmic operations of creation, conservation and consummation. But as in terms of the *trimūrti* or the 'Hindu trinity' Śiva is associated with the destruction of the universe,[80] this aspect of his role in the cosmic drama, namely that of the destroyer, is brought more closely into relation with the proofs of the existence of God in Śaiva theology than in other forms of Hindu theism.

If it be claimed that God exists because he brings about the destruction of the universe, then an objector could contend that 'we never witness the destruction of the entire world'. What we do witness is the destruction of parts of the universe. Can we, from this, conclude that the *whole* universe is also destroyed and therefore there is a destroyer who is God? The Śaiva thinkers have, quite ingeniously, drawn on a Buddhist argument here. The Buddhists maintain that there is no universe apart from and over and above its constituent parts. Now we *do see* its various parts ceasing to be: 'what is true of all the parts, with regard to their radical changeableness should also be true of the whole, which is nothing else than the sum-total of the parts'.[81]

One could counter thus: this only shows that parts of the universe are destructible; how do we deduce that everything in the universe and therefore the universe is destroyed simultaneously? Here the Śaiva Siddhāntin, the follower of one of the schools of philosophy associated with Śaivism, would argue that we

> find that various things belonging to the same genus exist at a particular time and are destroyed wholesale at another time. Seeds manifest their sprout during the spring; the sprouts which develop into plants are destroyed about the beginning of autumn. So, also the world, being material, is subject to similar origination and destruction. When the time comes for it, the world is manifested; again, when the time is ripe for it, the world is

> destroyed. May be, the intervals are prodigiously long. But the process is analogous.[82]

The second form of the argument takes the position that 'all things dissolve in the One that is above them'.[83] As everything dissolves into Śiva, he is above all.

IX

Before moving on to examine some grounds for disbelief in God as developed within Hindu philosophy, one might pause to reflect whether the Hindu grounds for belief in God contain any special features which are either only dimly anticipated or not anticipated at all in Western discussions on the subject. We have already noticed one such feature – the argument from destruction. But more generally one must begin with a preliminary consideration of Hindu polytheism.[84] The discussion of the proofs of the existence of God in the Western philosophy of religion assumes that there is only one such god, while Hinduism, on the face of it at least, countenances a host of gods; yet paradoxically there is little discussion of proofs of the existence of gods in Hindu philosophy. It is clear, then, that philosophical Hinduism is monotheistic and that Hindu polytheism in the present context is a red herring. Polymorphism or polynominalism should not be confused with polytheism.[85] Many Hindu texts can be quoted in support of monotheism.[86]

Two other considerations which affect the Hindu grounds for belief in God which were mentioned earlier may also be recalled: the independent existence of matter and the law of karma. It is easy to see how these beliefs could and did undermine theism in some ways – producing the ethical atheism and the spiritual materialism of the Sāṅkya school. The Pūrva Mīmāṁsā school of Hindu thought dispensed with God too on the maxim: 'The world itself suffices for itself.'[87] But at this point 'it should be added that, as . . . with the Sāṅkhya system, to deny the existence of God is not to discard the higher values; for the doctrine, unlike materialism, believes in surviving souls and in the theory of karma'.[88] Thus, unlike the Judeo-Christian tradition, denial of God does not automatically imply denial of either morality or salvation in Hinduism. With the rise of humanism in the West, it could be said that even in the West, theism and morality have been successfully sundered; but the other point remains unique to Hinduism, that spiritual salvation does not presuppose theism.

The fact remains, however, that Hindu thought is largely theistic and now, having cleared the decks, so to speak, we may once again inquire: in what way are the Hindu proofs of the existence of God uniquely Hindu?

It is commonplace to assert, as has already been done, that in the Hindu religious tradition theory and practice go hand in hand. Now it is true that, both in the Judeo-Christian and the Hindu religious traditions, the development of the formal proofs of the existence of God is far removed in time from the origin of the traditions. But the reasons for this probative lag seem to differ with the two traditions. In the case of the Judeo-Christian tradition, belief in God was so self-evident and central that there was little need to establish it. In the case of the Hindu religious tradition, God was not as central and hence no need was felt to establish it. This point is particularly important in relation to what was said earlier – that, in Hinduism, salvation is possible without God. The growth of theism in the Yoga school is an interesting case in point. It makes its initial appearance in Yoga because belief in God was thought to be practically helpful in attaining salvation; the theoretical proofs came later. Thus it has been pointed out that

> As distinguished from the Sāṅkhya, the Yoga is theistic. It admits the existence of God on both practical and theoretical grounds. Patañjali himself, however, has not felt the necessity of God for solving any theoretical problem of philosophy. For him God has more a practical value than a theoretical one. Devotion to God is considered to be of great practical value, inasmuch as it forms a part of the practice of yoga and is *one* of the means for the final attainment of samādhi-yoga or 'the restraint of the mind.' The subsequent commentators and interpreters of the Yoga evince also a theoretical interest in God and discuss more fully the speculative problems as to the nature of God and the proofs for the existence of God. Thus the Yoga system has come to have both a theoretical and a practical interest in the Divine Being.[89]

This pragmatic use of belief in God is a typically Hindu procedure in the sense that sometimes the tradition seems to set more store by the usefulness of a belief than by its truthfulness. But clearly this consideration, though important, must be excluded when the truthfulness of belief in the existence of God is at issue. The Judeo-Christian discussion on the matter does not stand to gain much by this clarification, but two other considerations promise to be less barren.

The first is the implication that belief in God may well represent a kind of natural religion[90] or theology. Hiriyanna is not the first to point out[91] that Udayana (the author of Nyāyakusumāñjali) 'implies in his prefatory remarks that the universality of belief in God is a sufficient proof of it'.[92] Can such a conclusion be sustained? Let the preface itself be examined:

> Now although with regard to that Being whom all men alike worship, whichever of the (four well-known) ends of man they may desire, – (thus the followers of the Upaniṣads [worship it] as the very knower, – the disciples of Kapila as the perfect first Wise, – those of Patañjali as Him who, untouched by pain, action, fruit or desert, having assumed a body in order to create, revealed the tradition of the Veda and is gracious to all living beings, – the Mahāpāśupatas as the Independent one, undefiled by vaidic [Vedic] or secular violations, – the Śáivas as Śiva, – the Vaiṣṇavas as Puruṣottama, – the followers of the Purāṇas as the great Father (Brahmā), – the Ceremonialists as the Soul of the sacrifice, – the Saugatas as the Omniscient, – the Jainas as the Unobstructed, – Mīmāṁsakas as Him who is pointed out as to be worshipped, *– the Cārvākas as Him who is established by the conventions of the world,* – the followers of the Nyāya as Him who is all that is said worthy of Him, – why farther detail? whom even the artizans themselves worship as the great artizan, Viśvakarman) – although, I say, with regard to that Being, the adorable Śiva, whom all recognise throughout the world as universally acknowledged like castes, families, family invocations of Agni, schools, social customs, &c., *how can there arise any doubt*? and what then is there to be ascertained? [my italic] (Introductory commentary I.3)[93]

Udayana seems to be forcing the point here by including the Cārvākas or Indian materialists, who may conventionally accept[94] but philosophically deny God and by regarding belief in the existence of God as self-evident. And as widespread acceptance of belief in the flatness of the earth at one time demonstrates, universal acceptance by itself cannot be proof of truth. Yet even modern thinkers have appealed to instinctive belief in God as proof of his existence.

But the point is helpful in one way. If a belief is so widely shared, should not the burden of proof, in respect of disproving it, rest with the opposing party? It is interesting that in

> trying to establish the existence of God, Udayana takes full advantage of the lack of any proof to the contrary. He devotes one whole chapter out of the five in the *Kusumāñjali* to the examination of this point and shows how none of the pramāṇas can be adduced to make out that God does not exist. This is no doubt a point of only dialectical value; but it cannot be denied that it has some force, especially against those that make much of the opposite fact that the existence of God can never be proved.[95]

Notes and References

1. Haridas Bhattacharyya ed, *The Cultural Heritage of India* vol. III (Calcutta: Ramakrishna Mission Institute of Culture, 1969 [first published 1937]) ch. 33.
2. Ibid., p. 544.
3. M. Hiriyanna, *The Essentials of Indian Philosophy* (London: George Allen & Unwin, 1949) pp. 89–90.
4. Ibid.
5. Haridas Bhattacharyya ed., op. cit., vol. III, p. 538.
6. See George Chemparathy, *An Indian Rational Theology: Introduction to Udayana's Nyāyakusumāñjali* (Vienna: Gerold, 1972) pp. 19–33.
7. Ibid.
8. Chandradhar Sharma, *A Critical Survey of Indian Philosophy* (London: Rider, 1960) pp. 209–10.
9. This convergence has been noticed by several scholars. Thus M. Hiriyanna comments after discussing the Nyāya position (*The Essentials of Indian Philosophy* p. 90): 'Here we find two of the common arguments for the existence of God: (1) The cosmological, which reasons from the fact that the world is an effect to a Being who can bring it into existence; and (2) the teleological, which reasons from the evidence of design or purpose found in the world to a just and prescient agent. From the vastness of the universe and its extraordinary diversity, it is deduced that its author must possess infinite power as well as infinite wisdom.' Other scholars even seem to rephrase Udayana in the light of the Western proofs of the existence of God. 'It is a characteristic of the Nyāya doctrine that it seeks to prove

even the existence of God. The chief of the arguments as set forth by Udayana are as follows: (1) The world which is an effect required an efficient cause. This cause must be equal to the task of creating the world both by knowledge as well as power. That is God. (2) There is orderliness in the created world. Natural phenomena do not constitute a chaotic mass. They reveal an intelligent design. As the author of this design, as the controller of the physical order, God must exist. (3) Just as there is a physical order, there is a moral order too, which consists in dispensing justice in accordance with desert. There must be one responsible for this as the moral governor. He is God. (4) There is also a negative proof. No anti-theist has so far proved the non-existence of God. No *pramāṇa* can be adduced to show that God does not exist.' (T. M. P. Mahadevan, *The Outlines of Hinduism* [Bombay: Chetana, 1971] p. 107).

10. John H. Hick, *Philosophy of Religion*, 3rd edn (Englewood Cliffs, New Jersey: Prentice-Hall, 1983) p. 20.
11. See David Hume, *Dialogues Concerning Natural Religion* (New York: Hafner, 1948). For a summary see John H. Hick, op. cit., pp. 25–6.
12. M. Hiriyanna, op. cit., p. 57.
13. Some scholars have suggested that Sāṅkhya may originally have been theistic and later assumed the classical atheistic form (see T. M. P. Mahadevan, *Outlines of Hinduism*, p. 116). For more on its theistic or atheistic character see Jadunath Sinha, *A History of Indian Philosophy*, vol. II (Calcutta: Central Book Agency, 1952) pp. 88–92.
14. Surendranath Dasgupta, *A History of Indian Philosophy*, vol. I (Delhi: Motilal Banarsidass, 1975 [first published by Cambridge University Press, 1922]) p. 325. For a possible limitation of this position see M. Hiriyanna, op. cit., pp. 126–7.
15. S. Radhakrishnan, *Indian Philosophy*, vol. II (London: George Allen & Unwin, 1927) p. 171.
16. Surendranath Dasgupta, op. cit., vol. I, p. 325.
17. Ibid., p. 326.
18. Chandradhar Sharma, op. cit., p. 174.
19. For Sanskrit text see M. R. Desai ed., *The Yoga-Sutras of Pantanjali* (Kolhapur: Desai Publication Trust, 1972); for translation see James Haughton Woods tr., *The Yoga-System of Patanjali* (Delhi: Motilal Banarsidass, 1966 [first published by Harvard University Press, 1914]); for another presentation see Sarvepalli Radhakrishnan and Charles A. Moore eds, *A Source Book of Indian Philosophy* (Princeton, New Jersey: Princeton University Press, 1971) p. 458.
20. M. Hiriyanna, *The Essentials of Indian Philosophy*, p. 125.
21. John H. Hick, op. cit., p. 16.
22. Ibid.
23. Satischandra Chatterjee and Dhirendramohan Datta, *An Introduction to Indian Philosophy* (University of Calcutta, 1968 [first published 1939]) p. 308.
24. T. M. P. Mahadevan, *Outlines of Hinduism*, pp. 129–30.
25. Sarvepalli Radhakrishnan and Charles A. Moore eds, *A Source Book of Indian Philosophy*, p. 458.

26. This may be a manifestation of a more general trend in the tradition in favour of revelation vis-à-vis reason; N. K. Devaraja, *Hinduism and Christianity* (New Delhi: Asia Publishing House, 1969) p. 51.
27. Ninian Smart, *Doctrine and Argument in Indian Philosophy* (London: George Allen & Unwin, 1964) pp. 149–50. Madhva (1199–1278) is another major theistic thinker of India.
28. Ninian Smart, *ibid.*, p. 154.
29. See Bharatan Kumarappa, *The Hindu Conception of the Deity as Culminating in Rāmānuja* (London: Luzac, 1934) p. 155.
30. Ibid., p. 156.
31. Ibid., pp. 153–5.
32. See ibid., p. 158.
33. Ibid., p. 156.
34. See Ibid., p. 156.
35. Ibid., p. 153.
36. Ibid., p. 159.
37. Ninian Smart, op. cit., p. 154.
38. P. N. Srinivasachari, *The Philosophy of Viśiṣṭadvaita* (Wheaton, Illinois: Adyar Library and Research Center, 1970 [first printed 1943]) p. 14.
39. Bharatan Kumarappa, op. cit., p. 162. Ninian Smart feels that the Nyāya school was able to 'produce apparently reasonable replies' to at least some of the above arguments (*Doctrine and Argument in Indian Philosophy*, pp. 155–6).
40. M. Hiriyanna, *Outlines of Indian Philosophy* (London: George Allen & Unwin, 1964 [first published 1932]) p. 258. See Ninian Smart (*Doctrine and Argument in Indian Philosophy*, pp. 150–1) on the relationship between omniscience and scripture. Also see Satischandra Chatterjee and Dhirendramohan Datta (*An Introduction to Indian Philosophy*, pp. 210–19) wherein it is pointed out (ibid., pp. 214–16, 218) that Nyāya too uses scriptural authority as one of the arguments to establish the existence of God, as was shown to be the case earlier with Udayana. It could be argued that this involves circular reasoning: Vedas are valid because they are the word of God; God exists because the Vedas say so. 'But that there is really no circular reasoning here becomes clear when we distinguish between the order of *knowledge* and the order of *existence*. In the order of existence, God is prior to the Vedas, and He reveals them. In the order of our knowledge, however, the Vedas are known first, and we rise from them to a knowledge of God. But for our knowledge of the Vedas, we need not be necessarily and absolutely dependent on God, since these may be learned from an eligible and efficient teacher. All reciprocal dependence is not reasoning in a circle. It is only when there is a reciprocal dependence with reference to the same order or within the same universe of discourse, that there arises the fallacy of reasoning in a circle. In the present case, however, the Vedas depend on God for their existence but not for their knowledge by us, while God depends on the Vedas for our knowledge of Him but not for His existence. So there is really no fallacy of reasoning in a circle.' (Ibid., p. 218).
41. Interestingly, just as Nyāya, while giving primacy to rational theism,

also uses the scripture as evidence, Vedānta, while giving primacy to scriptural authority as the basis of theism, also forges a connection between God and scripture. The view is 'common to all schools of Vedānta' that 'the Veda has had an author, viz. God; but it is not his work in the accepted sense of that word. Like everything else, the Veda also disappears at the end of a cycle; and God repeats it at the beginning of the next cycle, just as it was before, so that it may be regarded as eternal in the sense of in which a beginningless series of like things is. It is therefore really independent of God (*apauruṣeya*) in so far as its substance as well as its verbal form is concerned, although its propagation at the beginning of each cycle is due to him. It thus secures self-validity for the Veda.' (M. Hiriyanna, *The Essentials of Indian Philosophy*, p. 169). As distinguished from the above position, Nyāya 'ascribes the authorship of the Veda to God in the ordinary sense of the term' (ibid).

42. Satischandra Chatterjee and Dhirendramohan Datta, *An Introduction to Indian Philosophy*, p. 216.
43. Ibid.
44. Ibid.
45. Read 'Dollars'.
46. Satischandra Chatterjee and Dhirendramohan Datta, op. cit., p. 216.
47. Ibid.
48. Ibid. The actual statement again reads like an overstatement: 'The existence of a thing is to be known, if at all, through experience, direct or indirect.'
49. Ibid.
50. Ibid.
51. Ibid.
52. George Chemparathy, *An Indian Rational Theology: Introduction to Udayanas Nyāyakusumāñjali*, p. 73.
53. M. Hiriyanna, *The Essentials of Indian Philosophy*, p. 173.
54. P. N. Srinivasachari, *The Philosophy of Viśiṣṭadvaita*, p. 15.
55. S. Radhakrishnan, *Eastern Religions and Western Thought* (New York: Oxford University Press, 1959) pp. 22–3.
56. John H. Hick, *Philosophy of Religion*, p. 29.
57. G. P. Malalasekera, *Dictionary of Pāli Proper Names*, vol. II (London: Pali Text Society, 1960) p. 203.
58. *Māsaka* seems to refer to a kind of coin.
59. J. B. Horner (tr.), *The Book of the Discipline*, vol. V (London: Luzac, 1963) pp. 151–2.
60. Rammohun Roy, *The Precepts of Jesus* (Boston: Christian Register Office, 1828) pp. xviii–xix.
61. John H. Hick, op. cit., p. 30.
62. Ninian Smart, *Doctrine and Argument in Indian Philosophy*, p. 158.
63. Ibid., p. 150.
64. That is, the followers of Jainism, which, like Buddhism, is one of the ancient religions of India.
65. M. Hiriyanna, *The Essentials of Indian Philosophy*, p. 44.
66. Ibid., p. 45. M. Hiriyanna is pushing the point a little here. The

condition is only 'sometimes laid down' and the word *mahājana* could also mean 'masses' (see P. V. Kane, *History of Dharmaśāstra*, vol. V pt II [Poona: Bhandarkar Oriental Research Institute, 1977] p. 1271).

67. Pratima Bowes, *The Hindu Religious Tradition: A Philosophical Approach* (London: Routledge & Kegan Paul, 1977) p. 281.
68. John H. Hick, op. cit., pp. 28–9.
69. Ninian Smart, op. cit., pp. 152–3.
70. *Talks with Sri Ramana Maharshi* (Tiruvannamalai: Sri Ramanaramam, 1972) pp. 30–1.
71. Ninian Smart, op. cit., p. 153.
72. M. Hiriyanna, *The Essentials of Indian Philosophy*, pp. 48–9.
73. The following brief and perhaps even brilliant statement of the doctrine of karma may interest the reader. 'In short, the law of the conservation of energy is rigidly applied to the moral world. Every action, whether good or bad, must have its result for the doer. If in the present life a man is on the whole good, his next existence is better by just so much as his good deeds have outweighed his evil deeds. He becomes a great and noble man, or a king, or perhaps a god (the gods, like men, are subject to the law of transmigration). Conversely, a wicked man is reborn as a person of low position, or as an animal, or, in cases of exceptional depravity, he may fall to existence in hell. And all this is not carried out by decree of some omnipotent and sternly just Power. It is a natural law. It operates of itself just as much as the law of gravitation. It is therefore wholly dispassionate, neither merciful nor vindictive. It is absolutely inescapable; but at the same time it never cuts off hope. A man is what he has made himself; but by that same token he may make himself what he will. The soul tormented in the lowest hell may raise himself in time to the highest heaven, simply by doing right. Perfect justice is made the basic law of the universe. It is a principle of great moral grandeur and perfection.' (Franklin Edgerton, *The Bhagavadgītā* [Cambridge, Mass.: Harvard University Press, 1972] p. 123).
74. Karl H. Potter, *Presuppositions of India's Philosophies* (Englewood Cliffs, New Jersey: Prentice-Hall, 1963) p. 2.
75. Ibid.
76. Ibid., p. 3.
77. See Eliot Deutsch, *Advaita Vedānta: A Philosophical Reconstruction* (Honolulu: East-West Center Press, 1969) ch. 7.
78. See ibid., ch. 7; P. N. Srinivasachari, *The Philosophy of Viśiṣṭadvata*, p. 59, 147–9; but also see Sabapathy Kulandran, *Grace: A Comparative Study of the Doctrine in Christianity and Hinduism* (London: Lutterworth Press, 1964) p. 255.
79. See V. A. Devasenapathi, *Śaiva Siddhānta as Expounded in the Sīvajñana-Siddhiyar and Its Six Commentaries* (University of Madras, 1966) ch. III.
80. A. L. Basham, *The Wonder That Was India* (New York: Grove Press, 1954) pp. 310–11.
81. Mariasusai Dhavamony, *Love of God According to Śaiva Siddānta* (Oxford: Clarendon Press, 1971) p. 203.
82. V. A. Devasenapathi, op. cit., p. 78.

83. Mariasusai Dhavamony, op. cit., p. 205.
84. For perceptive discussions of Hindu polytheism see Pratima Bowes, *The Hindu Religious Tradition: A Philosophical Approach* (London: Routledge & Kegan Paul, 1977); Alain Daniélou, *Hindu Polytheism* (New York: Bollingen Foundation, 1964); Donald and Jean Johnson, *God and Gods in Hinduism* (New Delhi: Arnold–Heinemann India, 1972); and other works.
85. Haridas Bhattacharyya (ed.), *The Cultural Heritage of India*, p. 122.
86. S. Radhakrishnan, *The Hindu View of Life* (New York: Macmillan, 1927) p. 22.
87. M. Hiriyanna, *The Essentials of Indian Philosophy*, p. 135; also see T. M. P. Mahadevan, *Outlines of Hinduism*, p. 138.
88. M. Hiriyanna, *The Essentials of Indian Philosophy*, p. 135.
89. Satischandra Chatterjee and Dhirendramohan Datta, *An Introduction to Indian Philosophy*, p. 307.
90. Eric J. Sharpe, *Comparative Religion: A History* (London: Gerald Duckworth, 1975) p. 5.
91. The position in this respect has perhaps earlier been overstated by a scholar but his remarks are useful (Haridas Bhattacharyya (ed.), op. cit., vol. III, pp. 541–2): 'In the systems, both orthodox and heterodox, attempts have been made either to prove or to disprove the existence of God. The Cārvākas, as we have already noted, believe only in perception as the valid means of knowledge. Merit, life after death, heaven, hell, soul, and God are not objects of perception. So they do not exist. According to the Buddhists, a thing that has nowhere been perceived cannot exist. As God has not been perceived by anybody anywhere, He does not exist. According to the Jains, God's omniscience is not valid knowledge, because right knowledge is that which is produced only in the case of an object not known before. But as God knows everything, His knowledge is necessarily of known objects and hence untrue. So even if God exists, none can direct any faith to Him. According to the Sāṁkhya, there is no logical proof of the existence of God. The inherent teleology in Prakṛti is sufficient to explain creation, and the intervention of God is superfluous and unnecessary. The Mīmāṁsakas believe in the eternality of the Vedas. So the argument of the Naiyāyikas that God exists because He is the creator of the Vedas is not tenable. By the performance of religious rites one gets to heaven, the *summum bonum* of human aspiration. So, more than this, it is not necessary to conceive, nor can it be proved.

   The great Naiyāyika, Udayanācārya, who has written an elaborate thesis on the proofs of the existence of God in his famous treatise *Kusumāñjali*, has examined the foregoing arguments and found them wanting. At the beginning of his book, he says "What doubt can there be in God, experience of whom is admitted throughout the world?' So, any argument in support of His existence is unnecessary and redundant from the standpoint of the Naiyāyikas. But even then proofs of His existence have been adduced. Because, as Udayanācārya writes, "This logical consideration of God is tantamount to thinking (*manana*) about Him. It follows hearing (*śravaṇa*) about Him, and is undertaken as a form of worship (*upāsanā*)".'

92. M. Hiriyanna, *The Essentials of Indian Philosophy*, p. 92.
93. Sarvepalli Radhakrishnan and Charles A. Moore (eds), *A Source Book of Indian Philosophy*, p. 379.
94. E. B. Cowell and A. E. Gough (trs), *The Sarva-Darśana-Saṃgraha by Mādhava Ācārya* (London: Kegan Paul, Trench, Trübner, 1914) p. 4.
95. M. Hiriyanna, *Outlines of Indian Philosophy* (London: George Allen & Unwin, 1964 [first published 1932]) p. 243.

2

Grounds for Disbelief in God

The grounds for disbelief in God have been offered within the Indic religious tradition by the materialists, the Buddhists and the Jainas.[1] The arguments offered by the Buddhists and the Jainas need to be dealt with separately in the accounts of Buddhist and Jaina philosophies of religion.[2] In this chapter we shall present, in the main, the grounds for disbelief in God offered by the school of Indian thought known variously as the Lokāyata or the Cārvāka.[3] It may be added that the same school also offers grounds for disbelief in the soul, rebirth and so on, as well, but the present discussion will be confined to its arguments for disbelief in God.

The grounds for disbelief adduced by the Cārvākas[4] may be classified in various ways, but it is perhaps best to begin by indicating those arguments which seem to represent modern trends of thought.

THE MARXIST CRITIQUE OF RELIGION

Anticipations of the Marxist critique of religion can be easily detected in Cārvāka literature. It is clearly stated that religion and all that goes with it, namely, the concepts of scriptural authority, god, afterlife and so on, are merely devices used by a crafty priesthood to exploit the people. The well-known compendium of Indian thought, the Sarvadarśanasaṅgraha, offers the following summary of Cārvāka doctrines on this point.

> There is no heaven, no final liberation, nor any soul in another world; nor do the actions of the four castes, orders, etc. produce any real effect. The Agnihotra, the three Vedas, the ascetic's three staves and smearing one's self with ashes, were made by Nature as the livelihood of those destitute of knowledge and

> manliness. If a beast slain in the Jyotiṣṭoma rite will itself go to heaven, why then does not the sacrificer forthwith offer his own father? . . . If beings in heaven are gratified by our offering the Shrāddha here, then why not give the food down below to those who are standing on the house top? While life remains let a man live happily, let him feed on ghee (clarified butter) even though he runs in debt; when once the body becomes ashes, how can it ever return here? . . . (All the ceremonies are) a means of livelihood (for) Brāhmaṇas. The three authors of the Vedas were buffoons, knaves and demons.[5]

If, according to Marx, the criticism of religion is the beginning of all criticism, then the Indian materialists made a good start and this vein of Indian thought is being exploited by modern Marxist thinkers in India.[6]

The main merit of this critique of theism is that it shows how religion, and theistic religion in particular, can be used as an instrument of economic exploitation. But Luther saw that too. Does the abuse of the belief in God constitute adequate proof of his non-existence?

THE FREUDIAN CRITIQUE OF RELIGION

Although the Indian materialists anticipate the Marxian critique of religion, one key point needs to be borne in mind. For Marx, religion is identical with theism, but it was shown earlier that this is not necessarily the case with Hinduism. Hence the Indian materialist critique of religion is not confined to the concept of God and the constellation of beliefs surrounding it.

A similar caveat is in order while discussing the Freudian elements in the Indian materialist critique of religion. For Freud, religion was the collective neurosis of mankind and the key element in this neurosis was the suppression of libidinal instincts. The Indian materialist critique of religion is, however, quite candid on this point. Thus it is clearly said that 'one should enjoy the company of lustful young ladies'[7] and that 'licentious persons recite the Vedas only to conceal their weakness, they refer to the Yam(a) Yami Sukta to justify their illegal sexual relations and say that they are only following their holy scriptures. In this way some preach the practice of Niyoga (the) religious debauchery.'[8] It is further said that 'rituals are performed only to procure chances of drinking wine and copulation with (the) women other than wives'. Thus the Sautrāmaṇi sacrifice may be referred to 'wherein wine is drunk under a religious garb' and the Aśvamedha sacrifice as well 'wherein oral sex is considered as a part of the sacrifice'.[9]

There is also the absence of the critique of God as a father-figure in Indian materialist circles. It could however be argued that it is the guru rather than God, and the fact that guru is equated with God, which provides the Freudian clue here.

On the other hand there are some accounts vaguely reminiscent of the primal horde thesis of Freud. There is, for instance, the following dialogue between a king and his wife Kuntī in one of the famous epics of Hinduism:

> 'In the olden days, so we hear, the women went uncloistered, my lovely wife of the beautiful eyes; they were their own mistresses who took their pleasure where it pleased them. From childhood on they were faithless to their husbands, but yet not lawless, for such was the Law in the olden days. Even today the animal creatures still follow this hoary Law, without any passion or hatred. This anciently witnessed Law was honored by the great seers, and it still prevails among the Northern Kurus, Kuntī of the softly tapering thighs, for this is the eternal Law that favors women. But in the present world the present rule was laid down soon after – I shall tell you fully by whom and why, sweet-smiling wife!
>
> 'There was, so we hear, a great seer by the name of Uddālaka, and he had a hermit son who was called Śvetaketu. It was he, so we hear, who laid down this rule among humankind, in a fit of anger, lotus-eyed Kuntī – now hear why. Once, in full view of Śvetaketu and his father, a brahmin took Śvetaketu's mother by the hand and said, "Let us go". At this, the seer's son became indignant and infuriated, when he saw how his mother, as if by force, was being led away. But his father, on seeing him angered, said to Śvetaketu, "Do not be angry, son. This is the eternal Law. The women of all classes are uncloistered on earth. Just as the cows do, so do the creatures each in its class." Śvetaketu, the seer's son, did not condone the Law, and laid down the present rule for men and women on earth, for humans but not for other creatures, good lady. Ever since, we hear, this rule has stood. "From this day on", he ruled, "a woman's

> faithlessness to her husband shall be a sin equal to aborticide, an evil that shall bring on misery. Seducing a chaste and constant wife who is avowed to her husband shall also be a sin on earth. And a wife who is enjoined by her husband to conceive a child and refuses shall incur the same evil." Thus did Uddālaka's son Švetaketu forcibly lay down this rule of the Law in the olden days, my bashful wife.'[10]

But with Freud's own theory virtually discredited one must resist the temptation of reading too much into this account.[11]

THE LOGICAL CRITIQUE OF GOD

The most significant contribution which the Indian materialists make towards the critique of God is a logical one. It turns fundamentally on the following points: (a) that the concept of God is self-discrepant or palpably false; (b) that the existence of God cannot be logically inferred; (c) that even if it could be logically inferred, a prior epistemological issue must be faced: is inference a valid means of proving the existence of God?

God is often depicted in Hindu thought as (a) the cause of the world; (b) the revealer of divine scriptures and (c) the creator of language.

It is self-discrepant to portray God as the cause of the world for the following reasons. If God is a cause he must undergo modification; if God undergoes modification he cannot be an unchanging cause; if God is transcendent he cannot create; if he creates he cannot be transcendent; if God is eternal he cannot create (because he would have to be motionless); and if he creates he cannot be eternal. Finally if God is the cause of the world, who is the cause of God? And if God is uncaused why not make the same assumption about the universe.[12]

It is self-discrepant to portray God as the revealer of the Vedas, which are considered beginningless in the Hindu tradition. God can only know the scriptures after they are in existence.

> A person who became omniscient later on, how can he be called as 'knower of the beginningless scriptures,' for, these are two self-contradictory things. To be knower of the beginningless scriptures indicates that there must not be a time when the

> knower begins to know and to begin to know means that there is the beginning. A person who is supposed an omniscient one is a big hoax, for he tells a lie by proclaiming having those things simultaneously which cannot co-exist. To talk of 'beginningless scriptures' is sheer nonsense.
>
> If you say that god is proved by the statements of god, that, too, is absolutely wrong. To prove the existence of god by the statements of the so called beginningless scriptures and to prove the beginninglessness of the scriptures by the statements of the god is circulus in probando. So long as either of these two is not proved valid independently one cannot be a proof for the validity of the other.
>
> You maintain the validity of the scriptures on the witness of the 'omniscient' godmen or the god and on the other hand, you try to prove the existence of God with the help of those scriptures. How is it? There must be a third proof to prove the validity of both of them.[13]

Nor can God be regarded as the creator of language, for language is manmade. The materialists address those who regard language as a divine gift thus:

> If you say the relation of the word and the meaning thereof is god-made like the relation of fire and heat, then there must be the knowledge of the Vedas to all the creatures without deliberately knowing the meanings of the words. The heat of fire is felt by all without any sort of indoctrination but the meanings of the Vedas can not be known likewise. The relation of the word and the meaning thereof, is established by man-made tokens. No other theory except the 'theory of tokens' can maintain this relationship. Here the atheists are establishing that the language is a man-made phenomenon, not a god given boon.[14]

There is one logical option still open. One may try to *infer* the existence of God if it cannot be established otherwise. The materialists fire the following opening salvo:

> As we do not see an omniscient and a beginningless God similarly there is no god. If you say – 'You should infer the existence of god,' that is not right, for, without, at least partial, direct perception the inference is baseless and merely a child of one's imagination.

> In the total absence of inference there is no scope for the logos. When all the evidences are unable to prove the existence of the god, then all the praises and mythological accounts aimed at proving its existence are but useless and meaningless.[15]

The Cārvāka argument that the existence of God cannot be logically inferred needs to be examined carefully, because it has been carefully made and is based on the limitation of inferential procedures.

The discussion of the proofs, or otherwise, of the existence of God possesses a venerable lineage in the philosophy of religion[16] and the issue is far from closed.[17] Echoes of these discussions can also be heard in the history of Indian philosophy.[18] It is not the purpose of this section, however, either to penetrate more deeply into the Western discussions of the subject or to navigate more adroitly the turns the controversy takes in Indian philosophy. Its aim is to draw attention to and to elaborate a particular circumstance: that while many of the proofs of the existence of God in the Western philosophy of religion are based on inference, the Indian materialist school of philosophy, popularly known as the Cārvāka or the Lokāyata, raises fundamental objections to the application of inference *per se* to the issue of the question of the existence of God. It is our hope to show that the elaboration of this Indian materialist position parallels substantially the positivist critique of the existence of God.

One must begin by clearing the air, so to speak, for the Indian materialists have often been caricatured.[19] Their texts are lost[20] and their position has to be reconstructed from the statements of their opponents or by the putting together of stray references.[21] It is generally assumed that, while Western philosophy recognises two sources of knowledge – perception and inference,[22] Indian materialists 'admit only one source of valid knowledge – perception'.[23] The other Indian schools were quick to point out that the rejection of inference must be based on inference and made short work of their position.[24] However the deeper significance of their rejection of inference needs to be recognised.

> It is stated that the Cārvāka admits the validity of only one *pramāṇa* viz. perception, and rejects not only verbal testimony but also inference. This can only mean that the Indian materialist was aware of the lack of finality in reasoned conclusions, because all of them rest implicitly, if not explicitly, on some induc-

> tive truth which, though it may be highly probable, is never demonstrably certain. It is this high probability that explains the successful prediction which is often possible of future events, as in the case of the rising of the sun tomorrow (say) after it sets today. There is nothing strange about such a view of inferential knowledge. In fact, the Indian materialist is here only upholding a position that is quite familiar to the student of modern logic. To deny inference in any other sense would be absurd, since the denial itself would be a generalized conclusion like those to which he objects on the score of uncertainty.[25]

The argument may now be further developed in both Western and Indian terms. In Western terms it is best pursued along the distinction between induction and deduction. It is helpful to recognise here that the basis of inference is universal concomitance (*vyāpti*). The Indian materialist argues that neither mode of reasoning can yield the kind of general principle one is seeking.

> A general proposition may be true in perceived cases, but there is no guarantee that it will hold true even in unperceived cases. Deductive inference is vitiated by the fallacy of *petitio principii*. It is merely an argument in a circle since the conclusion is already contained in the major premise, the validity of which is not proved. Inductive inference undertakes to prove the validity of the major premise of deductive inference. But induction too is uncertain because it proceeds unwarrantedly from the known to the unknown. In order to distinguish true induction from simple enumeration, it is pointed out that the former, unlike the latter, is based on a causal relationship which means invariable association or *vyāpti*. *Vyāpti* therefore is the nerve of all inference. But the *Chārvāka* challenges this universal and invariable relationship of concomitance and regards it a mere guess-work.[26]

The point is clear. If we accept the argument by design, or the teleological argument, as one of the more favoured ones to demonstrate the existence of God,[27] then clearly the existence of the invisible designer is being inferred from the design. In the case of fire being inferred from smoke *both* are perceptible, but such is not the case here and hence the Indian materialists regard inference as unwarranted.

The next point must now relate to the roots of concomitance. In order for a general proposition to be inferentially established must we insist that causation between the two terms has to be established or would invariable concomitance suffice? The question is not very helpful, for both of these are rejected by Indian materialists as not ascertainable by perception.

> The principle of causation was rejected, because it was not supported by sensuous perception. Mere perception of two events which stand isolated and self-contained is not sufficient to establish between them a causal relation. To ascertain whether a given antecedent condition has the character of a true cause, it is really necessary to find out with certainty the elements of invariability and of relevancy involved in such a notion. But this certitude can never be arrived at. Universal propositions cannot be established by our limited perceptions. Perception presupposes actual contact of the object with the perceiving organ and is thus necessarily confined to the present. It is a case of here and now; it does not extend to the past or the future, and is thus unable to establish the universal connection of things. In other words, sense perception can give us only particular truths. But the knowledge of particular facts cannot give us knowledge that is universally true. Therefore perception cannot give us universal relations.[28]

It should be noted that the Indian materialists *do not* infer polytheism from the fact that only particular objects are perceived,[29] but rather abandon the inferability of anything about an invisible realm from a visible realm altogether.

The Indian materialist position can now be further advanced with the help of concepts drawn from the Indian, rather than the Western, philosophical tradition. Two points may be borne in mind at this stage: that Hindu philosophy in general admits of more than merely two sources of knowledge – perception and inference – admitted in the West. To these in a standard listing are added: (three), comparison (*upamāna*) and (four), verbal testimony (*śabda*).[30] The other point which needs to be borne in mind is that some Hindu thinkers often distinguish between two forms of perception: internal and external; the first involving the perception of subjective states, the latter of objective existents.

Now in the following remarks, based on the famous text, the Sarvadarśanasaṅgraha, the position of the Indian materialists is depicted as successively dismissing each means of knowledge as individually capable of generating a middle term, and hence creating grounds for inference. First, perception, both internal and external, is rejected. External perception occurs only in the present and, 'as there can never be such contact in the case of the past or the future, the universal proposition which was to embrace the invariable connections of the middle and the major terms in every case becomes impossible to be known.'[31] Internal perception is naturally ineffective, as it is not independent of observable relationships.[32] As for inference: 'Nor can inference be the means of the knowledge of the universal proposition, since in the case of the inference we should also require another inference to establish it, and so on, and hence would arise the fallacy of an *ad infinitum* retrogression.'[33] Thus inference is rejected as capable of generating inference. Comparison is similarly ineffective because it does not set out to achieve a universal proposition.[34] Nor need testimony be accepted as a source for a universal proposition, as the relation of fire and smoke will still hold if not testified to, if testimony is accepted as the only means of valid knowledge.[35]

Moreover, testimony as a means of knowledge really implies inference, as its correctness is inferred from the reliability of the source.[36]

The Indian materialist school also develops the point further. In discussions of inference within Hindu thought, it is sometimes described as 'two-fold – that which resolves a doubt in one's own mind (*svārtha*) and that which does it in another's (*parārtha*)'.[37] Now it seems to have been suggested by some that inference for oneself may be acceptable.[38] This is also contested by the Indian materialists on the ground that there is really no difference between the two. When a person iterates his own position it becomes 'another's' and when another iterates his position it becomes one's own and all the arguments against inference apply.[39]

It should be noted however that the rejection of inference by the Indian materialists was tempered with time. On being

severely attacked by its opponents, who maintained the authority of inference, it showed for the first time a leaning towards admitting inference as a source of knowledge. At first it said that, for practical purposes, probability was sufficient. At the sight of smoke rising from a spot, we have a sense of the probability of fire, and not of its certainty; this is enough for all

> practical purposes, and there is no need to assume the existence of a distinct kind of evidence called inference. When further pressed, this school accepted inference as a means to right knowledge, since it was useful in our daily life. But it rejected the form of inference proposed by the Buddhists and others as being impracticable for daily use. In other words, it divided inference into two classes – one class referring to the future and the other to the past. It accepted the second and rejected the first, the inference about what has never been perceived, as for example, the future world, God, and the soul.[40]

The following conclusions suggest themselves. The Indian materialists only acknowledged sensory perception as a means of valid knowledge. The fact that God could not be perceived through the senses constituted an adequate ground for disbelief in his existence. Even when inference as a source of knowledge was admitted in a limited way, it was always kept closely bound to perception. It is here I think that Indian materialist thought makes a contribution to the positivist critique of the existence of God. Historically it anticipates it, but philosophically it says something more significant. Let us take the case of smoke on the hill leading to the inference of the presence of fire. Smoke, the middle term, in perceivable and so is the hill, the minor term. What is not perceived is fire, the major term, but it is *perceivable* just as the hill and the smoke are.[41] In other words whereas the Western critique of the proofs of the existence of God have centred on whether such inference *is* right or not, the Indian materialist critique rests on the ground that it is not right to infer in the matter.

THE CHALLENGE OF MODERN SCIENCE

In the West, the development of modern science took place in a context of opposition to the Church.[42] The Copernican revolution in astronomy gave a rude shock to the anthropocentrism of the medieval church. The rise of Darwinism called the literal acceptance of the Genesis stories into question and in general the autonomous nature of the physical universe has now come to be accepted. These changes posed a threat to theism in the sense that the general body of prescientific ideas associated with theism was discredited. A more direct attack came through the questioning of miracles, for they were often cited as proof of the truths of revelation.[43] What is interesting from the Hindu point of view is the fact that the medieval world-view did in general prevail in India,[44] but with one major difference: Hindu theology had a very different notion from the Christian regarding the sphere in which revelation was to be regarded as authoritative.[45] This difference, it seems, has turned out to be of crucial importance in determining the relationship between Hinduism and science. The Hindu view that revelation applies only in the suprasensuous realm leaves the world open for investigation by scientific epistemological procedures without prejudice to religion. Miracles also play little role as proof of faith, though Hinduism abounds in them. Indeed when confronted with biblical miracles, the Hindus 'pointed out that the raising of Lazarus from the dead was unworthy of remark; their own religion had many more and astonishing miracles than this; and any true *yogi* could perform miracles today, while those of Christians were apparently finished'.[46] When the Hindu reformer Rammohun Roy (1772/74–1833), who admired the moral teachings of Jesus, published a translation of the Gospels he excluded the miracles.[47]

Thus scientific discoveries are seen as less shocking, and indeed often as quite consistent with the basic presuppositions of Hindu philosophy.[48] There is also the further point that perhaps Hindu philosophy has been more ontological than cosmological in its orientation by contrast with Christian theology.[49] The significance of the difference in its concept of revelation from the Christian however is perhaps the key to the fact that science does not seem to pose as great a challenge to Hindu theism, or to Hindu philosophy in general, as in the case of Christianity.

> In this context the principle accepted by the Mīmāmsā and the Vedānta schools, namely, that a religious scripture is not meant for giving us knowledge of perceptible, or inferable things is to be borne in mind. This would mean that in a religious scripture it is in vain to seek science or history, and that (as Śankara says clearly) where a scriptural passage contradicts an evident truth of perception, or inference, it is not really a scriptural passage but an *arthavāda* to be discarded.[50]

Murty even goes on to say that 'had European theologians followed this principle, much of the conflict between science and religion could have been avoided.' In any case the battle lines between science and religion can hardly be said to have been drawn in the context of the Hindu religious tradition.[51] According to some they are not even drawable.[52] Others have even gone further and see the Hindu philosophical world-view as not merely neutral but even congenial in relation to modern science.[53]

Notes and References

1. The situation in relation to the atheistic school of Sāṅkhya is more complex. Classical Sāṅkhya 'does not establish the non-existence of God. It only shows that Prakrti and Purusas are sufficient to explain this universe and therefore there is no reason for postulating a hypothesis of God. But some commentators have tried to repudiate the existence of God, while the later Sāṅkhya writers like Vijñānabhiksu have tried to revive the necessity for admitting God. Those who repudiate the existence of God give the following arguments: if God is affected by selfish motives, He is not free; if He is free, He will not create this world of pain and misery. Either God is unjust and cruel or He is not free and all-powerful. If He is determined by the law of Karma, He is not free; if not, He is a tyrant. Again, God being pure knowledge, this material world cannot spring from Him. The effects are implicitly contained in their cause and the material world, which is subject to change, requires an unintelligent and ever-changing cause and not a spiritual and immutable God. Again, the eternal existence of the Puruṣas is inconsistent with God. If they are the parts of God, they must have some divine power. If they are created by God, they are subject to destruction. Hence there is no God.' (Chandradhar Sharma, *A Critical Survey of Indian Philosophy* [London: Rider, 1960] pp. 164–5.)
2. For brief accounts see S. Radhakrishnan, *Indian Philosophy*, vol. I (London: George Allen & Unwin, 1923) pp. 329–32, 453–6.
3. As distinguished from Indian materialism in general; see Kewal Krishan Mittal, *Materialism in Indian Thought* (Delhi: Munshiram Manoharlal, 1974).
4. Some of the arguments for disbelief in God advanced by the Indian materialists are rather shallow and have been overlooked. For instance, it is argued that if God's words are unfailing why does he not fulfil the petitioner by merely saying 'yes'! Or that, because God is the dispenser of karma and therefore of my misery, he is my enemy without good cause, while, in the case of others at least, there is a cause underlying the enmity. See Dakshinaranjan Shastri, *Chārvāka-Shashti* (Indian Materialism) (Calcutta: Book Company, no date) pp. 37–8.
5. Chandradhar Sharma, *A Critical Survey of Indian Philosophy*, p. 42. For the full text in translation see Sarvepalli Radhakrishnan and Charles A. Moore (eds), *A Source Book of Indian Philosophy* (Princeton, New

Jersey: Princeton University Press, 1971) pp. 228–34. Also see Haridas Bhattacharyya (ed), *The Cultural Heritage of India*, vol. III (Calcutta: Ramakrishna Mission Institute of Culture, 1969 [first published 1937]) ch. 8; and Surendra Ajnat (ed.), *Old Testament of Indian Atheism* (Jullundur, India: Bheem Patrika Publications, 1978) pp. 139–40.

6. See Debiprasad Chattopadhyaya, *Lokāyata: A Study in Ancient Indian Materialism* (New Delhi: People's Publishing House, 1973); and other works.
7. Surendra Ajnat (ed.), *Old Testament of Indian Atheism*, p. 139.
8. Ibid., p. 137.
9. Ibid., p. 138.
10. J. A. B. van Buitenen (tr. & ed.), *The Mahābhārata* vol. I (University of Chicago Press, 1973) pp. 253–4.
11. John H. Hick, *Philosophy of Religion*, 3rd edn (Englewood Cliffs, New Jersey: Prentice-Hall, 1983) pp. 34–6.
12. See Surendra Ajnat, op. cit., pp. 123–4.
13. Ibid., pp. 113–15.
14. Ibid., p. 117.
15. Ibid., pp. 112–13.
16. See William P. Alston (ed.), *Religious Belief and Philosophical Thought: Readings in the Philosophy of Religion* (New York: Harcourt, Brace & World, 1963); John Hick (ed.), *Classical and Contemporary Readings in the Philosophy of Religion* (Englewood Cliffs, New Jersey: Prentice-Hall, 1964); Frederick Ferré, *Basic Modern Philosophy of Religion* (New York: Charles Scribner's Sons, 1967).
17. John H. Hick, *Philosophy of Religion*, p. 30.
18. See S. Radhakrishnan, *Indian Philosophy*, vol. II p. 165ff; Surendranath Dasgupta, *A History of Indian Philosophy*, vol. I (Delhi: Motilal Banarsidass, 1975 [first published by Cambridge University Press, 1922]) pp. 325–6.
19. M. Hiriyanna, *The Essentials of Indian Philosophy* (London: George Allen & Unwin, 1949) p. 57.
20. S. Radhakrishnan, op. cit., vol. I, p. 283.
21. Chandradhar Sharma, op. cit., pp. 40–1.
22. John H. Hick, *Philosophy of Religion*, pp. 57–8.
23. D. M. Datta, *The Six Ways of Knowing* (University of Calcutta, 1972) p. 19.
24. Satischandra Chatterjee and Dhirendramohan Datta, *An Introduction to Indian Philosophy* (University of Calcutta, 1960) pp. 78–9.
25. M. Hiriyanna, op. cit., pp. 57–8.
26. Chandradhar Sharma, op. cit., pp. 42–3.
27. John H. Hick, *Philosophy of Religion*, p. 23.
28. Haridas Bhattacharyya (ed.), *The Cultural Heritage of India*, vol. III (Calcutta: Ramakrishna Mission Institute of Culture, 1969) p. 173.
29. See K. Satchidananda Murty, *Revelation and Reason in Advaita Vedānta* (New York: Columbia University Press, 1959) p. 208.
30. T. M. P. Mahadevan, *Outlines of Hinduism* (Bombay: Chetana, 1971) p. 101.
31. Sarvepalli Radhakrishnan and Charles A. Moore (eds), *A Source Book of*

Indian Philosophy (Princeton, New Jersey: Princeton University Press, 1971) p. 231.
32. Ibid.
33. Ibid.
34. Haridas Bhattacharyya (ed.), op. cit., vol. III, p. 174.
35. Ibid.
36. Ibid.
37. M. Hiriyanna, *Outlines of Indian Philosophy* (London: George Allen & Unwin, 1964) p. 255.
38. Surendra Ajnat (ed.), *Old Testament of Indian Atheism*, pp. 84–5.
39. Ibid., p. 86.
40. Haridas Bhattacharyya (ed.), op. cit., vol. III, pp. 181–2.
41. Jadunath Sinha, *A History of Indian Philosophy*, vol. I (Calcutta: Sinha Publishing House, 1956) pp. 239–40.
42. See Andrew D. White, *A History of the Warfare of Science and Theology in Christendom* (New York: George Brazilier, 1955).
43. John H. Hick, *Philosophy of Religion*, pp. 35–9.
44. Ainslie T. Embree (ed.), *Alberuni's India* (New York: W. W. Norton, 1971) p. xv, 24–5.
45. N. K. Devaraja, *Hinduism and the Modern Age* (New Delhi: Islam and the Modern Age Society, 1975) pp. 69–70.
46. Will Durant, *Our Oriental Heritage* (New York: Simon and Schuster, 1942) p. 615.
47. Ajit Kumar Ray, *The Religious Ideas of Rammohun Roy* (New Delhi: Kanak Publications, 1976) p. 46.
48. Satischandra Chatterjee and Dhirendramohan Datta, *An Introduction to Indian Philosophy*, p. 23.
49. Ibid., p. 396; N. K. Devaraja, *Hinduism and Christianity* (New Delhi: Asia Publishing House, 1969) p. 106 fn. 27.
50. K. Satchidananda Murty, *Revelation and Reason in Advaita Vedānta* (New York: Columbia University Press, 1959) pp. 311–12.
51. See Alain Daniélou, *Hindu Polytheism* (New York: Bollingen Foundation, 1964) p. 13.
52. K. N. Devaraja, op. cit., pp. 114–15.
53. See F. S. C. Northrop, *Man, Nature and God* (New York: Simon and Schuster, 1962) ch. XVIII.

3

Hindu Theodicies: The Problem of Evil

I

Once belief in God is entertained, an issue is likely to arise sooner or later, and sooner rather than later, which has to do with the existence of evil. It was raised in the sixth century BC by the Buddha in relation to the Hindu god Brahmā:

> If Brahma is lord of the whole world and creator of the multitude of beings, then why (i) has he ordained misfortune in the world without making the whole world happy, or (ii) for what purpose has he made the world full of injustice, deceit, falsehood and conceit, or (iii) the lord of beings is evil in that he ordained injustice when there could have been justice.[1]

Or to put it in more modern terms:

> As a challenge to theism, the problem of evil has traditionally been posed in the form of a dilemma: if God is perfectly loving, God must wish to abolish all evil; if God is all-powerful, God must be able to abolish all evil. But evil exists; therefore God cannot be both omnipotent and perfectly loving.[2]

In other words, the following three statements need to be reconciled:

(1) God is omnipotent;
(2) God is benevolent;
(3) Evil exists.[3]

II

The problem of evil has been dealt with within the Hindu religious tradition in two ways: philosophically and mythologically. Given the nature of the present enterprise, it is the resources of Hindu philosophy which will be drawn upon in the rest of this chapter.[4]

III

One may begin by examining the concept of evil itself more closely. Some useful distinctions are drawn in Western studies of the subject. Augustine, for instance, distinguishes between evil that man *does* which is sin (*peccatum*) and the evil that man *suffers* which is punishment (*poena*).[5] Thus we 'usually speak of evil in two ways: first, when we say that someone has done evil; second, when someone has suffered something evil'.[6] The distinction sometimes helps in suggesting the right English word to use for the Sanskrit *pāpa* in Hindu texts.[7] John H. Hick identifies three referents of the term evil: (a) physical pain; (b) mental suffering; and (c) moral wickedness, noting that the 'last is one of the causes of the first two, for an enormous amount of human pain arises from mankind's inhumanity'.[8] He also goes on to distinguish between pain caused by human action and pain not caused by human action, but 'such natural causes as bacteria and earthquakes, storm, fire, lightning, flood, and drought'.[9] Arthur L. Herman also draws a triple distinction in relation to evil: subhuman evil (that is, in relation to animals); human evil and superhuman evil (in relation to angels).[10]

The purpose of the foregoing survey was to prepare the ground for bringing the concept of evil into proper relation to Hindu thought wherein, it seems, the kind of issues raised by the use of the word evil are raised by the use of the word *dukkha*. Interestingly *dukkha* is most clearly discussed in two of the non-theistic schools of Indian thought, Buddhism and Sāṅkhya. In Sāṅkhya, to stay within the orbit of Hindu philosophy, *dukkha* is explained thus:

> Our life on earth is a mixture of joys and sorrows. There are indeed many pleasures of life, and also many creatures who have a good share of them. But many more are the pains and

> sufferings of life and *all* living beings are more or less subject to them. Even if it be possible for any individual being to shun all other pains and miseries, it is impossible for him to evade the clutches of decay and death. Ordinarily, however, we are the victims of three kinds of pains, *viz.*, the ādhyātmika, ādhibhautika and ādhidaivika. The first is due to intra-organic causes like bodily disorders and mental affections. It includes both bodily and mental sufferings, such as fever and headache, the pangs of fear, anger, greed, etc. The second is produced by extra-organic natural causes like men, beasts, thorns, etc. Instances of this kind are found in cases of murder, snake-bite, prick of thorns and so forth. The third kind of suffering is caused by extra-organic supernatural causes, e.g., the pains inflicted by ghosts, demons, etc.[11]

It will be seen that, in the Western philosophy of religion, evil includes both natural and man-made catastrophes, but seems to exclude general dissatisfaction with life. In other words, from a Hindu point of view, the problem of evil is only a more acute form of the problem of suffering. A further point needs to be noted: the Hindu mind is also engaged by the fact of the differentiae constituting humanity and the iniquities that go with that. To move from the problem of evil to the problem of inequality is no doubt quite a leap, but the presence of inequality and thereby apparent iniquity provokes the Hindu mind to seek for an explanation which may not be unconnected with the question of evil, for often differences in spiritual merit or virtue could be said to account for differences of fortune.[12]

IV

It has sometimes been suggested that, in some forms of Hindu thought, evil or suffering possesses no reality and therefore the problem of evil does not really arise.[13] The reference is obviously to Advaita Vedānta, in which the experience of the world is sometimes regarded as similar to a dream and not absolutely real. It needs to be recognised that not all schools of Hindu thought regard the world as ultimately unreal and 'evil is real for those schools in which the world is real; and even for the other schools it is real as long as the world is real'.[14] It is interesting to discover that, in one of the popular texts of the Advaita Vedānta, it is the problem of suffering which drives the pupil to seek refuge with the Guru. The pupil exclaims (Vivekacūḍāmaṇi 40–1):

> How to cross this ocean of phenomenal existence, what is to be my fate, and which of the means should I adopt as to these I know nothing. Condescend to save me, O Lord, and describe at length how to put an end to the misery of this relative existence.
>
> As he speaks thus, tormented by the afflictions of the world – which is like a forest on fire – and seeking his protection, the saint eyes him with a glance softened with pity and spontaneously bids him give up all fear.[15]

Therefore the problem of evil or suffering must be treated as real. It is sometimes maintained, again, that according to the dicta of Advaita Vedānta, the universe is essentially dualistic and must, of necessity, consist of opposites, so that suffering is bound to exist along with joy. We live in a middle world.[16] This position, again, does not seem to answer the problem of evil, for to say that evil is relative does not mean that it is not real unless we define real as that which is not relative. But that real itself becomes some kind of an 'ideal'. Evil is relative in another sense – it is relational. The Holocaust was evil for the Jews, but the Nazis had a different opinion about it. It was nevertheless real – at least for the Jews. So just because evil is relational or relative does not make it empirically unreal. Now even the school of Advaita Vedānta, which maintains that ultimately there is only one single reality, accepts the existence of God at the penultimate level.[17] So the problem therefore is still with us: why is there evil given that God exists?

V

In order to present the Hindu response to the issue clearly one needs to distinguish between two issues: (a) what is the *cause* of evil and (b) what accounts for the *existence* of evil?

The cause of evil in Hindu thought is regularly connected with karma, and its logical corollary, the doctrine of rebirth. The doctrine and the manner in which it serves to explain evil may be briefly stated.

> Every action, whether good or bad, must have its result for the doer. If in the present life a man is on the whole good, his next existence is better by just so much as his good deeds have outweighed his evil deeds. He becomes a great and noble man, or a king, or perhaps a god (the gods, like men, are subject to the law of transmigration). Conversely, a wicked man is reborn as a person of low position, or as an animal, or, in cases of exceptional depravity, he may fall to existence in hell. And all this is not carried out by decree of some omnipotent and sternly just Power. It is a natural law. It operates of itself just as much as the law of gravitation. It is therefore wholly dispassionate, neither merciful nor vindictive. It is absolutely inescapable; but at the same time it never cuts off hope. A man is what he has made himself; but by that same token he may make himself what he will. The soul tormented in the lowest hell may raise himself in time to the highest heaven, simply by doing right. Perfect justice is made the basic law of the universe. It is a principle of great moral grandeur and perfection.[18]

This doctrine raises several questions which will be discussed in a subsequent chapter, but its relevance, as it relates to the present issue, is clear. Evil is caused, not by God, but by man. What applies to an individual applies, *mutatis mutandis*, to all individuals, to groups of individuals and to all sentient beings. Behind every evil suffered, there lies a prior evil deed which accounts for it and for which it is a retribution. The Adhyātma Rāmāyaṇa thus expounds its comprehensive working out of the doctrine:

> None can ever be the cause of fortune or misfortune of another. The *karman* which we have ourselves accumulated in the past, that alone is the cause of fortune and misfortune. To attribute one's fortune and misfortune to another is an error, as it is a vain pride to think: 'It is I who am the author of this,' for all beings are bound by the chain of their *karman*. If man fancies to himself that some beings are his friends, others his enemies or are indifferent to him, it is according to the *karman* that he has worked out himself. It is necessary, therefore, that man should bear with one mind his fortune and misfortune, which are only fruits of his own actions. He should say unto himself: 'I desire neither to obtain enjoyments nor to be deprived of them; whether I acquire them or not, it is just the same'; and thus he should not be a

slave. In whatever situation, whatever time, and for whatever reasons, man accomplishes an action, good or bad, he must submit to its consequences accordingly.

It is therefore in vain that he rejoices or is aggrieved of a happy or an unhappy event, because the decrees of Destiny are inevitable even for demons and gods. Man can never escape pleasure or pain, because his body, which is a product of his good or bad actions, is by nature transient. After pleasure pain, after pain pleasure; creatures cannot escape these two, as they cannot the succession of day and night. They are intimately associated as water and mud. It is, therefore, that Sages knowing that all is but illusion, remain steadfast and neither are aggrieved nor joyous for events unhappy and happy.[19]

VI

Most Hindus seem to find in the doctrince of karma an adequate answer to the problem of evil at the religious level, as distinguished from the philosophical. For them, notwithstanding the loose ends or frayed edges that may show up when the doctrine is examined microscopically through a philosophical lens, it provides a satisfactory explanation of the problem of evil. As M. Hiriyanna has observed:

> The law of karma accordingly is not a blind mechanical law, but is essentially ethical. It is this conviction that there are in reality no iniquities in life which explains the absence of any feeling of bitterness – so apt to follow in the wake of pain and sorrow – which is noticeable even among common people in India when any misfortune befalls them. They blame neither God nor their neighbour, but only themselves for it. In fact, this frame of mind, which belief in the karma doctrine produces, is one of the most wholesome among its consequences. Deussen refers thus to the case of a blind person whom he met once during his Indian tour: 'Not knowing that he had been blind from birth, I sympathized with him and asked by what unfortunate accident the loss of sight had come upon him. Immediately and without showing any sign of bitterness, the answer was ready to his lips, 'By some crime committed in a former birth'.[20]

It has also been suggested that the doctrine of karma and rebirth offers not merely a religiously satisfying, but a philosophically sound, solution to the problem of evil. Thus Arthur L. Herman maintains that the 'Indian doctrine of rebirth in one of its formulations (a basically Hindu notion)'[21] 'can yield what was heretofore proved to be doctrinally difficult for most European philosophers, *viz.* an acceptable philosophic solution to the problem of evil'.[22]

It will be shown in the rest of this chapter that even if this claim is correct, one is still left with a philosophical problem of evil in relation to God. This becomes clear once the issue is rephrased as follows: How is God to be related to karma? Those schools of Hindu thought who do not accept God may not have to face this issue but most of Hindu thought does accept the existence of God. The issue, therefore, cannot be sidetracked. What the widespread acceptance of the doctrine of karma within Hinduism really does to the issue is to change its formulation, for the *existence* of evil, apart from its *cause*, still remains an issue if both God and the doctrine of karma form parts of the same philosophical system.

We shall now see how the problem of evil in its new incarnation as the relationship between karma and God is dealt with in two schools of Hindu thought: (1) Nyāya and (2) Vedānta. The Vedānta school of Hindu thought, however, is characterised by the existence of major sub-schools and three of the better known among them will be discussed separately. These are the schools of Vedānta known as Advaita Vedānta (non-dualism), Viśiṣṭādvaita Vedānta ('qualified' monism)[23] and Dvaita Vedānta (dualism). Thus in effect four schools of Hindu thought will be discussed: Nyāya, Advaita Vedānta, Viśiṣṭādvaita Vedānta and Dvaita Vedānta.

VII

If the doctrine of karma is accepted as an adequate explanation of the problem of evil then, as it was pointed out earlier, it is philosophically neater to accept atheism as well. For even if God may not cause evil under the doctrine of karma, if we accept the existence of God, then he allows it to exist. Now if God is accepted as just and as the supervisor of the operation of karma then the problem of evil in relation to God can still be kept at bay. As the followers of the Nyāya school explain:

> Just as God is the efficient cause of the world, so He is the directive cause of the actions of all living beings. No creature, not even man, is absolutely free in his actions. He is relatively free, i.e., his actions are done by him under the direction and guidance of the Divine Being. Just as a wise and benevolent father directs his son to do certain things, according to his gifts, capacities and previous attainments, so God directs all living beings to do such actions and feel such natural consequences thereof as are consistent with their past conduct and character. While man is the efficient instrumental cause of his actions, God is their efficient directive cause (prayojaka kartā). Thus God is the moral governor of the world of living beings including ourselves, the impartial dispenser of the fruits of our actions (karmaphaladātā) and the supreme arbiter of our joys and sorrows.[24]

If, however, compassion is also regarded as a key attribute of God then can God still be absolved?

The Nyāya school thinks that God's compassion can be reconciled with the working of the 'law' of karma. Such a reconciliation is attempted by the versatile and erudite Hindu thinker of the ninth century AD known by the name of Vācaspati Miśra. His explanation contains several strands. One of them is that moral laws are by their nature immutable, but this does not really compromise God's omnipotence because 'moral law is rather the law of his own being and also of the being of individual selves.' So mercy cannot subvert it. Moreover, God's whole idea in creating the universe is to enable souls to work out their karma and move towards God-realisation. 'Suffering is not an unmitigated evil' either. It is 'a blessing in disguise' and a 'propaedeutic discipline and a necessary preparation' for the achievement of salvation.[25]

VIII

It should be pointed out at this stage that the various schools of Hindu thought also differ among themselves as to the proper way of reconciling the doctrine of karma with the existence of God, though the broad framework of the attempted solution is a shared one – namely, that there is no inherent contradiction here, that the 'law' of karma is itself part of God's nature, a sign of his grace, and that God cannot be blamed for the existence of evil either because of his nature or the nature of his creative activity. This last point may be pursued further as it indicates how the explanations of the philosophical schools interact.

God becomes implicated in karmic evil and in the problem of evil if he is involved in the process of creation on purpose; not to achieve any purpose of his own to be sure, but for the purpose of enabling the karmic destinities of various beings to be worked out, as was suggested earlier. Some other thinkers are of the view that God can be further distanced from evil by suggesting, as has been done in the Vedāntasūtras (II. I. 32–6), that 'creation is mere sport' to God. The point is thus elaborated by S. Radhakrishnan:

> There are inequalities among the souls; some are happy and others unhappy. Does it mean that the Divine has also the qualities of passion and malice? As there is so much pain in the world, are we to treat him as cruel also? For these reasons *Brahman* cannot be the cause of the world. The objections are not valid. The inequalities of creation are due to the merit and demerit of the creatures. They are not a fault for which the Lord is to blame. An analogy is given. As Parjanya, the giver of rain, is the common cause of the production of rice, barley and other plants, and the differences are due to the potentialities of the seeds themselves, even so God is the common cause of the creation while the differences are due to the merit and demerit of the individual souls.[26]

The argument needs to be understood carefully. When it is being stated that God has no purpose of his own in bringing the creation about, the question arises: then why does he do it? The answer: in sport. It is not implied that it may be fun for God, but a cruel joke for us, because the attitude of sport relates to God's attitude to his *own* activity in relation to the cosmic process.[27] A second answer is sometimes implied: the creative process is a demonstration of God's glory.

If however the real point is that God has no purpose of his *own* to achieve through creation, then, on the analogy of human beings, it could be argued that both the explanations 'for sport' and for 'glory' (or even in 'glorious sport' if we wish to combine the two) are open to question, as there can really be no motiveless activity. The motive behind sport is amusement to remove boredom and the motive behind demonstrating one's powers is to show them off.[28] So that in the end, according to Nyāya, really no explanation for creation 'can be offered beyond positing that it is God's nature' to create'.[29] Śaṅkara comes close to assuming this position when he compares the process of creation in relation to God with that of (unconscious?) breathing in relation to human beings.[30] 'Following the law of one's own nature' seems to be involved. It has been similarly argued that 'God is a dynamic principle and His dynamism is manifested in his cosmic activities; and no room is left for speculation as to why God should be dynamic. . . . The ultimate nature of things can be understood only from observation of their behaviour and not *a priori*.'[31] This Nyāya line finds some support in Vedānta also, when it is suggested that 'we cannot question why God's nature is what it is. We have to accept it.'[32]

This position, however, creates another problem. If God's nature as such is dynamic, then God to that extent becomes less of a personal God. For to the extent that God is inherently and not volitionally dynamic, to that extent the activity of creation becomes impersonal. Let us now try to see how the school of Advaita Vedānta tries to solve the problems associated with the reformulated problem of evil.

IX

The system of Advaita Vedānta ultimately traces evil in the world, at the individual level, to an ignorance of our own true nature. Such ignorance or nescience is called *avidyā* and in its absence the individual will not experience any evil. Therefore the problem of evil in the present context may be rephrased as follows: 'Why does evil or "ignorance" exist in the world at all?'[33] Or if evil exists on account of ignorance or *avidyā*, then 'What is its ontological source? Why are we its victims in the first place?'[34]

> The Advaitan's answer to these questions shows why they cannot be intelligibly asked. 'Knowledge and ignorance', Śaṅkara writes, 'cannot co-exist in the same individual, for they are contradictory like light and darkness.' Knowledge destroys ignorance, hence, from the standpoint of knowledge, there is no ignorance whose origin stands in question. And when in ignorance, one cannot establish a temporal origin to what is conceiv-

able only in time (as Kant was later to show in Western philosophy) or describe the process by which this ignorance ontologically comes to be.

> The Advaitin thus finds himself in *avidyā*; he seeks to understand its nature, to describe its operation, and to overcome it: he cannot tell us why it, or the mental processes which constitute it, is there in the first place. With respect to its ontological source, *avidyā* must necessarily be unintelligible.[35]

We may still want to know, notwithstanding the ontological unintelligibility of *avidyā*, when the process of involvement in *saṁsāra*, or the process of rebirths wherein evil befalls us, commenced; that is to say, when did we fall prey to karma? As Hiriyanna anticipates

> Here, no doubt, a question will be asked as to when the responsibility for what one does was *first* incurred. But such a question is really inadmissible, for it takes for granted that there was a time when the self was without any disposition whatsoever. Such a view of the self is an abstraction as that of a mere disposition which characterizes no one. The self, as ordinarily known to us, always means a self with a certain stock of dispositions; and this fact is indicated in Indian expositions by describing Karma as beginningless (*anādi*). It means that no matter how far back we trace the history of an individual, we will never arrive at a stage when he was devoid of all character. Thus at all stages it is self-determination; and the Karma doctrine does in no sense imply the imposition of any constraint from outside.[36]

We may now switch to the cosmic level and revert to the question of why God brings about the periodic appearance of the universe. Here we encounter the term *māyā*. In Advaita Vedānta, the sole reality of Brahman without any distinctions is stated to be the ultimate truth. What accounts for our perception of it as other than that is *māyā* and the result of *māyā*. 'Whenever we transform the impersonal into the personal, that is, when we make Brahman something or someone who cares, we bring about an association of the impersonal with *māyā*'[37] and we arrive at God or Īśvara. Once so affirmed,

> Īśvara's creative activity is properly seen as *līlā*, as a free, sport-

> ive activity. If it were seen otherwise, it would lead to the kind of irresolvable dualism that has so often dogged the course of Western theology. Logically, as pointed out by many a philosopher, one simply cannot have the full reality of a transcendent God and the full reality of the world. One must have either a limited God (subordinate in some sense to the world) or an unlimited Reality and an 'appearance-only' world. By conceiving of Īśvara's activity as *līlā*, the Advaitin is able to place Īśvara, as well as the world, under *māyā* and thereby retain the unqualified Reality of Brahman.[38]

We can now see the difference between God's *līlā* and its varying concepts in Nyāya and Advaita Vedānta. The *līlā* is real in Nyāya; it is ultimately not so in Advaita Vedānta.

X

In relation to the thought of Rāmānuja, 'How, it may be asked, if Brahman is perfect bliss, does pain afflict the individual self, which depends upon Him even as completely as the body depends on the soul?'[39] The answer here is the same as elsewhere, that all evil is to be traced 'to *karman* or the deeds of souls, and Brahman is not responsible for them'.[40] According to Rāmānuja however the soul is dependent on Brahman: then does not evil become dependent on Brahman by implication? The answer given is that the soul has the power of free choice so that 'Brahman is indeed perfect, and the soul depends on Him, but not to the extent of foregoing its individuality or involving Brahman in imperfections'.[41] Then one must now ask: to what extent is the soul independent in its actions and in what sense is it dependent on Brahman? The action takes place through the soul's volition, but with Brahman's permission. According to Rāmānuja

> the case is analogous to that of property of which two men are joint owners. If one of these wishes to transfer that property to a third person he cannot do so without the permission of his partner, but that that permission is given is after all his own doing, and hence the fruit of the action (reward or anything) properly belongs to him only.[42]

Kumarappa goes on to comment:

> Or, to borrow a parable from the New Testament, the action of the prodigal son in taking his share of the goods from his father and in wasting it in riotous living is one for which the son alone is responsible, although the father permitted it. So also it would appear that though without Brahman's permission the soul is impotent to act, the responsibility for the act always rests upon the soul who wills it.[43]

If this be accepted then two further questions arise: (a) inasmuch as Brahman dispenses good and evil, can the soul 'be freed from the accusation of having an evil nature'? and (b) if Brahman loves the soul, why does it *permit* it to commit evil?[44] The answer given to the first question is that Brahman's nature is just, not evil. Evil proceeds from the soul's deed. Moreover, the evil result of evil deeds is not merely punitive, but redemptive as well.[45] Brahman permits evil because Brahman does not wish to interfere with the soul's freedom of choice.[46] Thus we find that

> By throwing the blame of evil ultimately on the souls themselves, Rāmānuja seeks to preserve the perfection and love of the Supreme Being. The chief difficulty of the theory is to explain how souls which are eternally parts of the Supremely perfect Brahman, ever came to desire what is evil. Rāmānuja adopts *the device of his predecessors to get over the difficulty by declaring that karman is beginningless* [my italic]; but this is no solution for it is merely to accept evil desires on the part of souls as somehow an ultimate fact. Nevertheless it is to Rāmānuja's credit that he sought systematically to maintain the perfection of Brahman as against the imperfections of the world. The solution that he offers to the problem of evil is not new, for the view that *karma* explains all the sufferings of *saṁsāra* is, as we saw, common to most of his predecessors. But his merit lies in attempting to make clear the exact relation in which the perfect Brahman stands to the deeds of souls.[47]

XI

We have considered the Nyāya solution to the problem of Karmic evil. We have also considered the solutions suggested by Śaṅkara

(Advaita Vedānta) and Rāmānuja (Viśiṣṭādvaita Vedānta). Let us now consider the solution offered by Madhva (Dvaita Vedānta). The problem is posed with sharp clarity by Vyāsa Rāya, an exponent of the school, thus:

> The question here is whether the causality of all things is proper to Viṣṇu or not. To resolve that we shall have to decide whether or not His causality of happiness and misery leads to His being unfair and cruel. This question can be decided only if we determine whether He acts without conforming with the karma of souls, or in conformity with it. And that problem can be determined only if we ascertain whether karma's capacity is independent of God, or whether, because of His supremacy, it is dependent on Him. To solve this difficulty we must make certain whether, granting karma's dependence on God, the partiality and harshness that lies in causing happiness and grief, which befalls the soul in conformity with the eternally existent capacity of the karma dependent on God – whether this partiality or harshness is blamable precisely because it is that, or because it contravenes the authority of the Veda (the impersonally originant Law of morality, which strongly condemns such behavior, and which declares that virtue leads to happiness and vice to pain).[48]

After a detailed discussion of various dissenting views it is concluded that 'unless we accept an innate aptitude (for good or evil) that is beginningless (and is not caused by God), the charges of partiality and callousness will be difficult to controvert'.[49] The Dvaita school basically criticises the other three schools for either making God's attitude too impersonal (Advaita), or too removed (Viśiṣṭādvaita), or too general (Nyāya), in relating evil actions to evil results. According to the Dvaita school God himself is the direct particular author of specific results and if they happen to be evil it is entirely because of the soul's *karma*.

Notes and References

1. Quoted in Gunapala Dharmasiri, *A Buddhist Critique of the Christian Concept of God* (Colombo: Lake House Investments, 1974) p. 55.
2. John H. Hick, *Philosophy of Religion*, 3rd edn (Englewood Cliffs, New Jersey: Prentice-Hall, 1983) pp. 40–1.

3. This is a modified form of the formulation by Arthur L. Herman, *The Problem of Evil and Indian Thought* (Delhi: Motilal Banarsidass, 1976) p. 3.
4. For the theodical elements in Hindu mythology see Wendy Doniger O'Flaherty, *The Origins of Evil in Hindu Mythology* (Berkeley: University of California Press, 1976). For theodicy in Hindu philosophy see Arthur L. Herman, *The Problem of Evil and Indian Thought*.
5. Arthur L. Herman, *The Problem of Evil and Indian Thought*, p. 15.
6. Quoted, ibid.
7. See R. C. Zaehner, *The Bhagavadgītā* (London: Oxford University Press, 1969) p. 292.
8. John H. Hick, op. cit., p. 40.
9. Ibid.
10. Arthur L. Herman, op. cit., pp. 21–2.
11. Satischandra Chatterjee and Dhirendramohan Datta, *An Introduction to Indian Philosophy* (University of Calcutta, 1968) pp. 279–80.
12. Charles A. Moore (ed.), *The Indian Mind* (Honolulu: University of Hawaii Press, 1967) p. 337.
13. Arthur L. Herman, op. cit., p. 246.
14. Satischandra Chatterjee and Dhirendramohan Datta, op. cit., p. 195.
15. Swami Madhavananda (ed.), *Vivekachudamani of Shri Shankaracharya* (Calcutta: Advaita Ashrama, 1966) pp. 15–16.
16. Huston Smith, *The Religions of Man* (New York: Harper & Row, 1958) p. 72.
17. Eliot Deutsch, *Advaita Vedānta: A Philosophical Reconstruction* (Honolulu: East-West Center Press, 1969) p. 43.
18. Franklin Edgerton (tr. & int.), *The Bhagavad Gītā* (Cambridge, Massachusetts: Harvard University Press, 1972 [first published 1944]) p. 123. For another statement of the doctrine see M. Hiriyanna, *The Essentials of Indian Philosophy* (London: George Allen & Unwin, 1949) pp. 48–9.
19. Louis Renou (ed.), *Hinduism* (New York: George Brazilier, 1962) p. 197.
20. M. Hiriyanna, *The Essentials of Indian Philosophy*, pp. 48–9.
21. Arthur L. Herman, op. cit., p. 5.
22. Ibid., p. 1.
23. The expression 'qualified monism' is a misnomer but is employed here as a concession to popular usage; see Arvind Sharma, *Viśiṣtādvaita Vedānta: A Study* (New Delhi: Heritage Publishers, 1978) pp. 15–19.
24. Satischandra Chatterjee & Dhirendramohan Datta, op. cit., p. 210.
25. Haridas Bhattacharyya (ed.), *The Cultural Heritage of India*, vol. III (Calcutta: Ramakrishna Mission Institute of Culture, 1969 [first published 1937]), pp. 112–13.
26. S. Radhakrishnan, *The Brahma Sūtra* (London: George Allen & Unwin, 1960) p. 363.
27. For a fuller discussion see Arthur L. Herman, *The Problem of Evil and Indian Thought*, p. 164ff.
28. See Haridas Bhattacharyya (ed.), op. cit., vol. III, pp. 113–14.
29. Ibid., p. 114.
30. S. Radhakrishnan, *The Brahma Sūtra*, p. 362.

31. Haridas Bhattacharyya (ed.), op. cit., vol. III, p. 114.
32. S. Radhakrishnan, *The Brahma Sūtra*, p. 362.
33. Eliot Deutsch and J. A. B. van Buitenen, *A Source Book of Advaita Vedānta* (Honolulu: The University Press of Hawaii, 1971) p. 76.
34. Eliot Deutsch, *Advaita Vedānta: A Philosophical Reconstruction*, p. 85.
35. Ibid., p. 85.
36. M. Hiriyanna, *The Essentials of Indian Philosophy*, pp. 47–8.
37. Eliot Deutsch, *Advaita Vedānta: A Philosophical Reconstruction*, p. 28.
38. Ibid., p. 44.
39. Bharatan Kumarappa, *The Hindu Conception of the Deity as Culminating in Rāmānuja* (London: Luzac, 1934) p. 270.
40. Ibid., p. 271.
41. Ibid., p. 272.
42. Quoted, ibid., p. 273.
43. Ibid.
44. Ibid., pp. 274–6.
45. Ibid., p. 275.
46. Ibid., p. 276.
47. Ibid., p. 277.
48. José Pereira (ed.), *Hindu Theology: A Reader* (New York: Image Books, 1976) p. 150.
49. Ibid., p. 156.

4

Christian Views of Revelation in a Hindu Context

I

According to modern thinking, 'Christian thought contains two very different understandings of the nature of revelation and, as a result, two different conceptions of faith (as the human reception of revelation), of the Bible (as a medium of revelation) and of theology (as discourse based upon revelation)'.[1] These two different understandings may, for convenience, be referred to as the propositional and the non-propositional views of revelation.

THE PROPOSITIONAL VIEW OF REVELATION

This view of revelation involves the following main points.

(1) That 'the content of revelation is a body of truths expressed in statements or propositions'.
(2) That 'faith is a supernatural virtue whereby, inspired and assisted by the grace of God, we believe the things that he has revealed are true'.
(3) That 'the Bible is the place where those truths are authoritatively written down'.
(4) That a distinction may be drawn between natural and revealed theology.[2]

Let us now consider this propositional view in relation to the Hindu religious tradition. It may be helpful to begin at the bottom, to take the last point first and proceed upwards. The application of the distinction between natural and revealed theology has already been discussed in a previous chapter. With respect to the Bible being an authoritatively written down record, it should be pointed out that the Vedas, though authoritative, have been written down only in recent times. The earliest manuscript dates to the 15th century AD and there are accounts of some earlier attempts to commit it to writing, but the Vedic tradition has essentially been an oral tradition. Faith, as the proper response to revelation and even to tradition, is widely attested to in Hindu literature. Thus the Bhagavadgītā (XVIII.71) declares that he who listens to it 'with faith, and not murmuring against it' obtains the fair worlds of men of virtuous deeds.[3] The ṚgVeda contains a hymn devoted to faith (X.151),[4] but it should be noted that faith applies more to works in Hinduism than to the text. In a very significant passage of the Bhagavadgītā a question is raised about the results of acts performed with faith, but *without* conforming to the scriptural injunctions (XVI.1) The answer brings out the intricate relationship between faith, works and revelation which, though basically of the same type as in Christianity, displays a much more developed typology. It would be tedious to consider the matter in detail here, as virtually the whole of the seventeenth chapter of the Gītā is devoted to it. Moreover, as such an investigation has already been undertaken by K. L. Seshagiri Rao, his conclusions are presented below. In this passage the word *śraddhā* corresponds to faith:

> (i) To speak of *śraddhā* in a categorical way is not sensible. *Śraddhā* is not a uniform category. It is individual and dynamic. It is a subjective attitude. It differs from person to person according to the proportional strength of the *guṇas* in each. A person's *śraddhā* depends on his *sattva*, individual nature (which is due to his *saṁskāras*); it moulds his being, and his being in turn moulds his *śraddhā*. So we can speak of *śraddhā* only with reference to a person's nature – his choice, taste and temperament.
> (ii) Although *śraddhā* is a subjective attitude, it is not entirely subjective. Its references are beyond itself. It has reference to (1) some objective goal that is aspired after; (2) the means that are relied upon to reach the goal; and (3) the *śāstra* that prescribes (1) and (2). These factors influence the quality of the subjective attitude. In view of these, it is possible to speak of certain typical manifestations of *śraddhā*. The *Gītā* speaks of three types of *śraddha* – *sāttvikī*, *rājasī* and *tāmasī*. This classification however, is diagnostic and not prescriptive.

> (iii) *Śraddhā* is possible only in embodied beings, that is, those who are under the influence of the *guṇas* of *prakṛti*.
> (iv) Scriptures are for the guidance of embodied beings. In the absence of the guidance of the scriptures, or of one who is well-versed in the scriptures, there is no way of knowing or approaching the transcendent.[5]

It is clear that unlike the Christian case, 'faith' is not uniquely related to God in Hinduism, nor is it uniform in its nature or operation. Nevertheless it is in relation to God that faith is increasingly spoken of as the Hindu religious environment turned theistic, although while in the Christian case it 'is at once an affirmation of truth and affirmation to the truth affirmed', in the Hindu case 'it almost entirely occupies the latter attitude'.[6]

The role of God in relation to faith in Hindu and Christian thought, however, must be examined further. For while it is true that God may help one acquire faith in revelation, it is not always true in Hinduism to say that the 'divinely authenticated truths' were revealed by him. The following situations are represented within the range of Hindu thought in this respect: (a) that the truths are not revealed by God at all; (b) that the truths are *not* revealed so much as proclaimed by God as creator; (c) that the truths are indeed revealed by God. The basic difficulty here is caused by the development of the view within Hinduism that the *Vedas* are *apauruṣeya*, that is to say, not the work of *any* author, God or man, but have been forever self-existent: 'There is no need to postulate a God as the author of the Veda, for the Veda is eternal,' like the universe, according to a particular school of Hindu thought (*Mīmāṁsā*). Significantly, this school did not subscribe to the standard Hindu view of periodic creation and dissolution of the universe, as it might interfere with its cherished doctrine of the eternality of the Vedas. Even those schools such as those of Vedānta, which did not completely accept the Mīmāṁsā idea, did not completely abandon it either, and evolved the second position on which the views of the monists coincide with those of the theists.

> The advaitin, unlike the Mīmāṁsaka, holds that the Veda has had an author, viz. God; but it is not his work in the accepted sense of that word. Like everything else, the Veda also disappears at the end of a cycle; and God repeats it at the beginning of

> the next cycle, just as it was before, so that it may be regarded as eternal in the sense in which a beginningless series of like things is. It is therefore really independent of God (*apauruṣeya*) in so far as its substance as well as its verbal form is concerned, although its propagation at the beginning of each cycle is due to him. It thus secures self-validity for the Veda, without subscribing to the palpably unconvincing theory of the Mīmāṁsā that it is self-existent and eternal.[7]

The third position is adopted by the Nyāya school of Hindu philosophy, whose attitudes often accord with those of Christianity. According to this school, 'all knowledge derived from the Vedas is valid, for the Vedas are uttered by Īśvara himself. The Vedas give us right knowledge not of itself, but because they came out as the utterances of the infallible Īśvara.'[8]

One may now turn to the matter of the content of the Vedas. Truth therein is no doubt seen as expressed in statements, but it might be useful here to distinguish between two kinds of statements: (a) those which enjoin ritual action; and (b) those which impart information about Brahman. The Hindu religious tradition, that is, that part of it which bases itself most centrally on the Vedas was divided on the question of whether (a) or (b) constitute the primary content of revelation. Ultimately those who took the (b) position prevailed. It so happens that propositional statements of type (a) abound in the earlier sections of the Vedas and of type (b) in the later, so that the schools involved in the process of rationally investigating the content of revelation (*mīmāṁsā*) came to be known respectively as the schools of *pūrva-mīmāṁsā* and *uttara-mīmāṁsā* as the words *pūrva* and *uttara* signify 'former' and 'latter'.

In other words the Hindu religious tradition accepts the propositional view of revelation but differs on the question of which propositions really count. In this respect the attitude of the Christians towards the Old and the New Testaments of the Bible is comparable. Just as for the Christians, unlike the Jews, the Old Testament has been superseded by the New Testament, similarly for the Vedāntins the former sections of the Vedas have been superseded by the latter, but not so for the Mīmāṁsakas (Pūrvamīmāṁsakas). (A terminological point may be made here. When the word Mīmāṁsā is used by itself it refers to the Pūrvamīmāṁsakas as distinguished from the Vedāntins. When the word Mīmāṁsā is used to *include* the Vedāntins then that school is called Uttaramīmāṁsā; and the Mīmāṁsā school is called Pūrvamīmāṁsā.)

We may now revert to the discussion of which propositional statements are regarded as significant by which school. Not only does the Mīmāṁsā school regard the former section of the Vedas as primary, but even here, it regards only directive propositions as constituting the message of the revelation. That is to say, the authority of revelation is primarily concerned with one's duties.

> To give a contrastive example, the orthodox Exegetes would reject most of the Bible as Revelation: most of it they would classify as *itihāsa* or *purāṇa*, 'stories about things past,' describing events which were accessible to perception and hence require only the authority of perception; but, for example, the chapters dealing with the Law in Deuteronomy would be considered Revelation in the true sense, since here rules are laid down and results are set forth which escape human perception and inference.[9]

The Vedāntins, by contrast, take a different position. Their position may be succinctly stated: only those propositions of the Veda are really meaningful which deal with the nature of Brahman and its realisation, not those which deal with ritual and its performance. As statements dealing with ritual (*karmakāṇḍa*) preponderate in the earlier sections of the Veda and those dealing with knowledge (*jñānakāṇḍa*) in the later, the controversy between the 'ritualists' and the 'gnostics' boils down to the relative assessment of the respective parts.

> It is taken for granted tht *karmakāṇḍa* indeed defines the principle of authority in injunctions of acts to be done, but Vedānta declines on the one hand that the Upaniṣads embody an injunction (for instance, that Brahman or the self must be studied and known, or that the world must be dephenomenalized) and declines on the other hand that if the Upaniṣads bear on no injunction they have simply the limited authoritative standing of a discussion. The consensus of the Vedānta is that in the Upaniṣads significant and authoritative statements are made concerning the nature of Brahman.[10]

THE NON-PROPOSITIONAL VIEW OF REVELATION

According to the non-propositional view of revelation, for which the more technical term of Heilsgeschichtliche view is used in Christian circles, revelation consists not of a body of doctrine but of the actual action of God in history itself.[11] It contains the following points of emphasis:

(1) 'the content of revelation is not a body of truths about God, but God coming within the orbit of human history';[12]
(2) 'theological propositions as such are not revealed but represent human attempts to understand the significance of revelatory events';[13]
(3) The question arises: If God does disclose himself, why does he not do so in 'an unambiguous manner'? It is in response to this ambiguity that faith plays its role in the non-propositional view of revelation, in which faith is conceived as 'a voluntary recognition of God's activity in human history, [and] consists of seeing, apperceiving, or interpreting events in a special way';[14]
(4) With faith, a divine pattern is seen in events which could also otherwise be seen as possessing no such pattern, as in the interpretation of God's action in the history of Israel.[15] It is as if 'two different orders or levels of significance are experienced within the same situation; this is what happens when the religious mind experiences events both as occurring within human history and as mediating the presence and activity of God'.[16]

The non-propositional view of revelation within Hinduism is perhaps best illustrated with the help of an incident from the life of Mahatma Gandhi (1869–1948). When one of his sons fell ill with typhoid and pneumonia the doctor recommended eggs and chicken broth. Gandhi was a strict vegetarian and with the approval of his ten-year-old son decided not to follow the doctor's orders but try hydropathic treatment instead. Gandhi knew that he was playing with his son's life and was assailed with doubts but persisted in his course in the hope that 'God would surely be pleased to see that I was giving the same treatment to my son as I would give myself.'[17] He also reflected that 'the thread of life was in the hands of God. Why not trust it to Him and in His name go on with what I thought was the right treatment.'[18] Gandhi applied the treatment. It was night and he was tired. He put the son in the care of his wife and went for a walk to refresh himself. 'It was about ten o'clock. Very few pedestrians were out. Plunged in deep thought, I scarcely looked at them. 'My honour is in Thy keeping oh Lord, in this hour of trial,' I repeated to myself. *Ramanama* was on my lips. After a short time I returned, my heart beating within my breast.'[19]

By the time Gandhi returned the fever had broken. His son made a full recovery. Gandhi concludes his narrative here with the remark:

> Who can say whether his recovery was due to God's grace, or to hydropathy, or to careful dietary [sic] and nursing? Let everyone decide according to his own faith. For my part I was sure that God had saved my honour, and that belief remains unaltered to this day.[20]

This is, of course, not a case of God coming within the orbit of human history. But it is a case of God entering the orbit of a human life. God also spoke to Gandhi through the inner voice in Gandhi's self-understanding and Gandhi saw God acting in history as the drama of the Indian Independence Movement unfolded in the twentieth century.

THE PROPOSITIONAL AND NON-PROPOSITIONAL VIEWS OF REVELATION IN CHRISTIANITY IN RELATION TO HINDUISM

We may begin by reminding ourselves of the simple point that the propositional view of revelation relates to divinely authenticated statements and the non-propositional view of revelation to divinely inspired events. Now in the case of Christianity both of these approaches are applied to the same corpus – the Bible. It will now be suggested that in Hinduism we have two different bodies of sacred literature representing these two approaches to revelation. The two different bodies of literature are the *śruti* and the *smṛti*. The propositional view of revelation applies to the *śruti* or the Vedas. The non-propositional view of revelation applies to the *smṛti*, a body of sacred books other than the Vedas. It is interesting that though the Hindu religious tradition maintains a fairly formal distinction between the two, and though its doctrinal position does not seem to lack a definite philosophical basis, new insights are supplied by the Christian theological distinction between the propositional and the non-propositional views of revelation.

First of all, what is *śruti* and what is *smṛti*?. One may begin by distinguishing between the two. The traditional position on the distinction between *śruti* and *smṛti* may be stated as follows:

> The foundational Scriptures of the Hindus are the Vedas. They are usually designated '*Śruti*,' while all the other scriptural texts go under the omnibus term '*Smṛti*'. The authority of the *Śruti* is primary, while that of the *Smṛti* is secondary. *Śruti* literally means what is heard, and *Smṛti* means what is remembered. *Śruti* is revelation; *Smṛti* is tradition. As between the two, *Śruti* is primary because it is a form of direct experience, where *Smṛti* is secondary, since it is a recollection of that experience.[21]

Now a few words in explanation of first the *śruti* and then the *smṛti*. The *śruti* is explained as follows:

> The Hindus believe that the Vedas which constitute *Śruti* are not compositions of any human mind. The Vedas are eternal (*nitya*) and impersonal (*apauruṣeya*). They are the breath of God, eternal truths revealed to the great *ṛṣis* of yore. The word '*ṛṣi*' is significant. It means a seer, from *dṛś* to see. The *ṛṣis* saw the truths or heard them. Hence the Vedas are what are heard (*Śruti*).[22]

And the following explanation is provided for *smṛtis*:

> Next in importance to *Śruti* are the *Smṛtis* or secondary scriptures. '*Smṛti*' is a word which is so elastic that it includes a variety of works on religious duty and philosophy. Besides the books which are specifically called *Smṛti*, there are the *Itihāsas*, *Purāṇas*, *Āgamas*, the *Darśana* literature and treatises and poems written in the popular languages. All these may be called *Smṛtis* because they draw inspiration from the Veda and regard the Veda as the final authority.[23]

If this traditional explanation is examined closely it is clear that it really tries to interpret *smṛti* in the light of the *śruti*. There is clear evidence to indicate, for instance, that some of the *smṛtis* were Un-vedic (Manusmṛti XII.95); the very passage tries to bring them in line with the Vedas.[24] The meaning of the term *smṛti* itself is also not quite fixed.[25]

It will now be suggested that the *śruti* is the repository of propositional revelation; that the *smṛti* is the repository of non-propositional revelation and that one of the tasks of Hindu hermeneutics has been to keep the two aligned.

It has already been shown, one hopes with sufficient clarity, that the Vedas or the *śruti* represent a propositional view of revelation. It is *śabda-pramāṇa*; its statements have probative value as consisting of propositional testimony about suprasensuous matters. It remains to be shown that the *smṛtis* represent non-propositional revelation.

The *smṛtis* typically fall into the following categories: (a) Dharmaśāstras or Law Books; (2) Itihāsas or the Great Epics of the Rāmāyaṇa and the Mahābhārata; (c) Purānas, dealing with the life accounts of the various gods and so on; (d) Āgamas or bodies of literature dealing with sectarian ritual; and (e) Darśana literature or philosophical works.

It might appear on the face of it that the law-books could not be regarded as non-propositional revelation; if anything, like Leviticus, they should be viewed as propositional revelation, unless of clearly human authorship. A closer look however reveals a rather different picture. No less than twenty *dharmaśāstras* are well known: how does one account for this proliferation? It is best to regard these law-books as revealed law acting itself out in history; the injunctions of the Vedas unfolding themselves within the realm of history. This human and theological reaction and adjustment to the irruption of divine law in the history of Hinduism is embodied in the *dharmaśāstras*, a fact clearly recognisable both objectively in history[26] and within the tradition as well, as in the dictum: 'There are different Smṛtis for different times.'[27]

The case for the great epics of the Rāmāyaṇa and the Mahābhārata as non-propositional revelation is both straightforward and more significant. The story of the incarnation of Rāma as contained in the Rāmāyaṇa[28] is too well-known to require elaboration. The work is clearly concerned with 'God coming within the orbit of human experience by acting in history', although some scholars tend to dismiss it as a mere myth.[29] Whether it is to be treated as myth or history is a consideration that itself creates room for 'that uncompelled response that theology calls faith.' The Mahābhārata, and within it the Bhagavadgītā, is similarly concerned with the god Kṛṣṇa coming into the orbit of human history, at least religious history, as perceived by the believers.[30] The Bhāgavata Purāṇa[31] develops the theme and the theological tension even further. The Purāṇas are replete with accounts of gods acting in the life of the devotees or in 'human history'. In fact they pose acutely the problem of faith as 'voluntary recognition of God's activity in human history' as some of this activity is, on the face of it, rather scandalous, and modern interpreters of Hinduism have had to explain these accounts acceptably. There is the account, for instance, of Kṛṣṇa as a child stealing the clothes of milkmaids bathing in the river, in the Bhāgavata Purāṇa.

> While the child of six was one day wandering along, as He would, a number of Gopís were bathing nude in the river, having cast aside their cloths – as they should not have done, that being against the law and showing carelessness of woman [sic] modesty. Leaving their garments on the bank they had plunged into the river. The child of six saw this with the eye of insight, and He gathered up their cloths and climbed up a tree near by, carrying them with Him, and threw them around His own shoulders and waited to see what would chance. The water was bitterly cold and the Gopís were shivering; but they did not like to come out of it before the clear steady eyes of the child. And He called them to come and get the garments they had thrown off; and as they hesitated the baby lips told them that they had sinned against God by immodestly casting aside the garments that should have been worn, and must therefore expiate their sin by coming and taking from His hands that which they had cast aside. They came and worshipped, and He gave them back their robes. An immoral story, with a child of six as the central figure! It is spoken of as though he were a full grown man, insulting the modesty of women. The Gopís were Rishis, and the Lord, the Supreme, as a babe is teaching them a lesson. But there is more than that; there is a profound occult lesson below the story – a story repeated over and over again in different forms – and it is this: that when the soul is approaching the supreme Lord at one great stage of initiation, it has to pass

> through a great ordeal; stripped of everything on which it has hitherto relied, stripped of everything that is not of its inner Self, deprived of all external aid, of all external protection, of all external covering, the soul itself, in its own inherent life, must stand naked and alone with nothing to rely on, save the life of the Self within it.[32]

In order to understand the significance of Āgama literature the Western reader must begin by overcoming his resistance to image-worship, for the consecrated image is regarded by the worshipper as the living God and therefore God is seen as actually present.[33] For a tradition whose theology has been at least aniconic, if not iconoclastic, it might be hard to see how non-propositional revelation may occur in an iconic form. Yet for the worshipper God has been brought into the orbit of human life in a rather visual manner. In some forms of theistic Hinduism, God in this form is known as *arcā* (image), while he is also known as interacting in cosmic history through other forms such as *vyūha*, or as immanent or as an incarnation as in the case of Rāma and Kṛṣṇa. The idol is the concrete presence of God in the life of the devotee and 'the belief is that God descends into the idol and makes it divinely alive so that he may be easily accessible to his devotees. A great South Indian savant has made the following comparisons in this respect; 'the attempt to comprehend the transcendent form is like getting water from the other world for quenching thirst; the *Vyūha* form is like the legendary ocean of milk which also is not easy of access; the immanent form is like subterranean water which is not readily available to a thirsty man although it is right underneath his feet; the incarnated forms are like the floods that inundate the country for a while but do not last long; and the *arcā* is like the . . . [still] pool from which anyone anytime could slake his thirst'.[34]

It will be easily seen that the doctrine of incarnation or *avatāra* has a prominent role to play in non-propositional revelation in the context of Hinduism. There are, of course, some important differences. There is only one incarnation in Christianity and several in Hinduism; in Christianity the incarnation is full man and full God, whereas it tends towards the 'docetic heresy' in Hinduism; and in Christianity the 'doctrine of Incarnation involves the claim that the moral (but not the metaphysical) attributes of God have been embodied, so far as this is possible, in a finite human life namely that of Christ'.[35] The distinction typically drawn in Hinduism is between an incarnation which exhibits divine attributes only partially (*aṁśa*) and one which does so fully (*pūrṇa*). Thus the doctrinal positions within Hinduism and Christianity on incarnation do not tally,[36] but family resemblance is hard to ignore. A great deal of debate centres on the question of whether the Hindu incarnations are 'myths,' while that of Jesus Christ is 'history,'[37] but, as pointed out earlier, if this fact itself is made a matter of faith then the convergence between the non-propositional view of revelation and the Hindu view of incarnation becomes more marked.

The one class of Smṛti literature difficult to fit into the category of a non-propositional view of revelation is the literature of the philosophical tradition of India which is naturally propositional. There is a genuine problem here though its force could be somewhat reduced either by suggesting: (a) that the individual thinkers are representing tradition and not revelation; or (b) by maintaining that the tradition is itself a form of extended propositional revelation, like the tradition of Oral Law in Judaism and the Roman Catholic view that 'it also accepts and venerates traditions concerned with faith and morals as having been received orally from Christ or inspired by the Holy Spirit and continuously preserved in the Catholic Church'.[38] But these considerations would put the material in the category of propositional revelation *unless* the interpreters are seen as incarnations of gods or earlier gurus moving within the ambit of human experience. There is, indeed, some evidence to be found in support of this.[39]

II

At this stage one further point needs to be considered. In the earlier section the Christian categories of propositional and non-propositional views of revelation were applied to the Hindu religious tradition. But is there any evidence to show that the Hindus ever tended to treat the Śruti and the Smṛti *both* as revelation, even if Śruti came to be regarded as revelation par excellence?

Although the standard position within Hinduism doubtless equates Śruti with revelation and Smṛti with tradition, virtually every phase of the history of Hinduism provides some evidence that the term revelatior was either actually or tentatively extended to include what we call tradition.

The earliest piece of evidence comes from the Upaniṣads themselves, wherein no distinction is drawn between the Vedas and the Itihāsas, Purānas and so on, in a famous passage (Bṛhadāraṇyaka 4.5.11):

> It is – as, from a fire laid with damp fuel, clouds of smoke separately issue forth, so, lo, verily, from this great Being (*bhūta*) has been breathed forth that which is Rig-Veda, Yajur-Veda, Sāma-Veda, [Hymns] of the Atharvans and Angirases, Legend (*itihāsa*), Ancient Lore (*purāṇa*), Sciences (*vidyā*), Mystic Doctrines (*upaniṣads*), Verses (*śloka*), Aphorisms (*sūtra*), Explanations (*anuvyākhyāna*), Commentaries (*vydkhyāna*), sacrifice, oblation, food, drink, this world and the other, and all beings. From it, indeed, have all these been breathed forth.[40]

In the classical, as distinguished from the Vedic period of Hindu history, the exegetes occasionally distinguished between the words Śruti and Veda, using the former word for revelation and the word Veda to represent one form of it – revelation too, it would appear, of the propositional kind. Evidence on this point is provided by Kullūka Bhaṭṭa, a commentator on the famous Law Book of Manu who is placed in the thirteenth century AD. Kullūka Bhaṭṭa seems to include Tantrism as a form of revelation, which was a quarternary development in Hinduism, if the Smṛti and the Purāṇas are regarded respectively as secondary and tertiary developments.[41]

In medieval times the tendency to extend the scope of revelation seems to have persisted. An important clue is provided by the development of the concept of *ubhayavedānta* in Tamilnadu. The word Vedānta belongs to the corpus of revealed literature in Hinduism, so there is little room for doubt that the term *ubhayavedānta* stands for dual revelation. The condition in which this concept developed is itself highly suggestive. By the time the devotional movement gained strength in Tamilnadu, Sanskritic Brahmanical culture had already been established there for some time. In this culture the Veda, and especially its last section, the Vedānta, constituted the revelation. In the meantime a body of devotional poetry dealing with the personal experience of the devotees with Viṣṇu in their own lives had taken shape. One can clearly detect elements of the non-propositional view of revelation here. The collected corpus of the Tamil songs of poet-saints is known as the *Nālāyira-Prabandham,* of which perhaps the best known is the Tiruvāymoḷi of Nammāḷvar. Rāmānuja placed this body of devotional literature on a par with the Upaniṣads. The concept of Ubhayavedānta refers to this fact of the simultaneous acceptance of these two bodies of literature as equally authoritative by Rāmānuja. However, merely to say that here we have an integration of the propositional view of revelation (*vedānta*) with the non-propositional view as represented by the Nālāyira-Prabandham is somewhat simplistic, for two reasons. First, Rāmānuja as a 'philosopher-saint'

> established the truths of Viśiṣṭādvaita as embodied in the *Vedānta-sūtra-s* and, at the same time, thought of each Adhikaraṇa as a *brahmānubhava* or experience of the Brahman. As a saint-philosopher he intuited the truths of *Tiruvāymoḷi* and gave a critical exposition of the experiences of the Āḷvār-s by showing their logical coherence. As a saint he contacted God and as a philosopher he proved the truths of spiritual experience.[42]

In this respect we revert to the Christian situation, as both the propositional and the non-propositional views of revelation were being directed towards the *same* text. However, and this is the second point, the Indologist could raise the objection that Rāmānuja used the Brahmasūtra, which though a member of the triple canon of Vedānta, is not a revealed work like the Upaniṣads in the integrative process. It is clear, however, that the Upaniṣads were involved in the process.[43] The points mentioned above should not obscure the basic point that the boundaries of revelation were being extended.

In the light of this historical background it is not surprising that in modern times we find advocates of the opinion that revelation should be extended to include even other bodies of non-Sanskrit sacred Hindu literature.

> To instance but a few, the *Tēvāram* and the *Tiruvācakam* are well-known among the hymns of the Śaiva saints of South India; the Vaiṣṇavas have correspondingly the *Divyaprabandham* and other devotional songs; the Caitanya movement and the songs of Tagore are responsible for the enrichment of Bengali devotional literature; the songs of Kabīr, the *Abhaṅgas* of the Mahārāṣṭra saints, the *Rāmāyaṇa* of Tulasi Dās are all outpourings of God-intoxicated souls. If the essentials of Hinduism have found a place, difficult to dislodge, in the homes of even the

lowliest and the last in this vast country, it is not a little due to these devotional poems in the languages of the people. To all of them the name 'Veda' may be given, for has not the Veda itself declared that the Vedas are many, unending (*anantā vai vedāh*)?[44]

Notes and References

1. John H. Hick, *Philosophy of Religion*, 3rd edn (Englewood Cliffs, New Jersey: Prentice-Hall, 1983) p. 60.
2. Ibid., p. 60, 61.
3. Franklin Edgerton (tr.), *The Bhagavadgītā*, pt I (Cambridge, Massachusetts: Harvard University Press, 1946) p. 177.
4. Sarvepalli Radhakrishnan and Charles A. Moore, *A Source Book of Indian Philosophy* (Princeton, New Jersey: Princeton University Press, 1971) p. 36.
5. K. L. Seshagiri Rao, *The Concept of Śraddhā* (Paliala: Roy Publishers, 1971) p. 164.
6. Nicol Macnicol, *Indian Theism from the Vedic to the Muhammadan Period* (London: Oxford University Press, 1915) p. 217.
7. M. Hiriyanna, *The Essentials of Indian Philosophy* (London: George Allen & Unwin, 1949) p. 169.
8. Surendranath Dasgupta, *A History of Indian Philosophy*, vol. I (Delhi: Motilal Banarsidass, 1975 [first published by Cambridge University Press, 1922]) p. 355.
9. Eliot Deutsch and J. A. B. van Buitenen, *A Source Book of Advaita Vedānta* (Honolulu: The University Press of Hawaii, 1971) p. 6.
10. Ibid., p. 7.
11. John H. Hick, op. cit., p. 69.
12. Ibid.
13. Ibid.
14. Ibid.
15. Bernhard W. Anderson, *The Living World of the Old Testament*, 3rd edn (London: Longman, 1975) pp. 72–4.
16. John H. Hick, op. cit., p. 70.
17. M. K. Gandhi, (tr. Mahadev Desai), *The Story of My Experiments with Truth*, (Washington, DC: Public Affairs Press, 1948) pp. 303–4.
18. Ibid., p. 304.
19. Ibid.
20. Ibid., p. 305.
21. T. M. P. Mahadevan, *Outlines of Hinduism* (Bombay: Chetana, 1971) p. 28.
22. Ibid., p. 29.
23. Ibid., p. 31.
24. Whether to treat Buddhist texts as *smrtis* or not and in what sense long remained an issue; see K. Satchidananda Murty, *Revelation and Reason*

in Advaita Vedānta (New York: Columbia University Press, 1959) pp. 216, 228, 230, 233ff.

25. Pandurang Vaman Kane, *History of Dharmaśāstra*, vol. v, pt II (Poona: Bhandarkar Oriental Research Institute, 1977) p. 1257ff. On Buddhist texts as *smṛtis* see pp. 1260, 1263, 1275.
26. Ibid., vol. v, pt II, p. 1269, etc.
27. T. M. P. Mahadevan, op. cit., p. 33. This statement is itself contained in a *smṛti* (Parāśarasmṛti I.24).
28. See Hari Prasad Shastri (tr.), *The Rāmayana of Valmiki* (London: Shantisadan, 1953–1959); for a popular account see R. K. Narayan, *The Ramayana* (New York: Penguin Books, 1977).
29. A. L. Basham, *The Wonder That Was India* (New York: Taplinger Publishing Company, 1967) p. 415.
30. R. C. Zaehner, *Hinduism* (London: Oxford University Press, 1966) pp. 91–3.
31. Thomas J. Hopkins, *The Hindu Religious Tradition* (Belmont, California: Dickenson Publishing Company, 1971) p. 102ff.
32. See Ainslie T. Embree (ed.), *The Hindu Tradition* (New York: Modern Library, 1966) p. 323.
33. Wm Theodore de Bary (ed.), *Sources of Indian Tradition*, vol. I (New York: Columbia University Press, 1958) pp. 335–6.
34. T. M. P. Mahadevan, op. cit., p. 194.
35. John H. Hick, *Philosophy of Religion*, p. 82.
36. See Geoffrey Parrinder, *Avatar and Incarnation* (London: Faber and Faber, 1970).
37. Hendrick Kraemer, *World Cultures and World Religions: The Coming Dialogue* (London: Lutterworth Press, 1960) p. 375.
38. John H. Hick, op. cit., p. 61.
39. See K. Satchidananda Murty, *Revelation and Reason in Advaita Vedānta* (New York: Columbia University Press, 1959) pp. 232–7.
40. Robert Ernest Hume (tr.), *The Thirteen Principal Upanishads* (Oxford University Press, 1968 [first published 1921]) p. 146.
41. James Hastings (ed.), *Encyclopaedia of Religion and Ethics*, vol. XII (New York: Charles Scribner's Sons, 1922) p. 193. One assumes that the word *tantra* has been used by Kullūka Bhaṭṭa in its common connotation and that he is reflecting an earlier tradition.
42. P. N. Srinivasachari, *The Philosophy of Viśiṣṭādvaita* (Wheaton, Illinois: Adyar Library and Research Center, 1970) p. 432.
43. Ibid., p. 531.
44. T. M. P. Mahadevan, op. cit., p. 39.

5

Religious Language

I

THE KEY ELEMENT IN LANGUAGE

Religious language, like all language, consists of verbal statements or propositions. These verbal statements or propositions are syntactically conjoined units. But one may ask:

> what is the nature of the information which such syntactically conjoined words convey? It cannot be merely the meanings of the various terms, because they are already known and so are only remembered at the time. It is some particular relation among the things denoted by the actual words forming the sentence. When we say 'The book is on the table,' it is a specific relation between the table and the book that is made known to the listener. The relation in this specific form is not the meaning of any single word used in the sentence, the preposition 'on' signifying only location in general; it is none the less known. Hence the import of a proposition is commonly stated to be *relation* (*saṁsarga*); and this holds good of the logically valid proposition as of that which is not.[1]

All language, therefore, is relational. But at this point an issue arises in Hindu thought which is perhaps not reflected in Western philosophy of religion to the same extent: although itself relational, can religious language only convey a relational sense? Can it also convey an 'impartite and non-relational sense', that is, refer to the Absolute which is totally free of all relations? This is a subject of controversy among the theistic and the absolutistic schools in Hinduism. In an earlier chapter a line from the Taittirīya Upaniṣad on Brahman (or the ultimate reality as conceived in Hinduism) was cited and the controversy just referred to actually crystallises around it.

This question arises particularly in connection with the definability of Brahman, and specifically in the context of the

> interpretation of the Upaniṣadic text, *'Satyam Jñānam Anantam Brahma'* which gives the definition of Brahman as 'Truth, Knowledge and Infinitude'. The main issue is whether in this text the terms in question denote the very *svarūpa* of Brahman or its characteristics. The Advaitin maintains the former view while the Viśiṣṭādvaitin holds the latter. The chief argument of the Advaitin for adopting the above view is that a sentence in which the terms are found in apposition (*sāmānādhi-karaṇya*) conveys an impartite and non-relational sense. Thus, for instance, in the judgment 'He (is) that Devadatta' the two terms 'He' and 'Devadatta' which stand in apposition do convey the idea of one individual. In other words, a sentence conveys the idea of one entity only when all its constituent terms denote one and the same thing. Accordingly, the Upaniṣadic text in question is understood to mean that Brahman is Truth, Knowledge and Infinitude and not that it is possessed of these three characteristics.[2]

It was indicated earlier that, according to theistic Hinduism, Brahman *possesses* these qualities and it is not the case that it *is* these qualities. That is to say, God is a person, or is at least personal if the former term has anthropomorphic overtones. We cannot pursue this interesting point further here,[3] except to note that the issue as such does not seem to arise in the Western philosophy of religion because of its predominantly theistic nature.

II

THE NATURE OF RELIGIOUS LANGUAGE

All Hindu thinkers are agreed that religious language belongs to a category by itself, though modern Hindu thinkers articulate this position more clearly for a modern audience. Thus it is said:

> Symbolisation is necessary for all communication, and perhaps for all thinking; for it is through symbols that man seeks to hold and make permanent the flux of events, which constitutes his experience. Language is a system of symbols, . . . language is not homogeneous, but has many levels. Science is one such level

> of language, while poetry is another. The mistake often made by critics of religion is to think that scientific language is adequate to deal with all types of experience. There are certain fundamental types of experience which cannot be treated by scientific language; and religious experience, which arises from the encounter of man with God, has given rise to a symbolism of its own.[4]

If, however, all language is symbolic, then what does the *uniquely* symbolic nature of religious language consist of?

In this respect the Thomistic explanation by analogy has met with approval in Hindu circles,[5] although the exact manner in which the result is achieved is explained somewhat differently in Hindu thought. Moreover, this discussion of analogy in the Thomistic sense is carried out in the sphere of linguistic theory rather than theology. The discussion of analogy is covered under the general topic of *lakṣaṇā*[6] and, despite much debate,

> it is clear that the various schools of thought in India were unanimous in accepting that in a transfer there must be some kind of relation between the primary and the actual referents. The secondary meaning is resorted to when the primary meaning is found incompatible with the context. This secondary meaning is not got immediately and directly from the word, but only through the primary meaning. The knowledge of the actual referent arises only indirectly; first we understand the primary meaning of the word; when this is found unsuitable in the context, the meaning is transferred to something related to the primary sense.[7]

It is easy to see how the operation here resembles the use of the analogical approach as distinguished from the univocal and the equivocal.[8] Thus in the expression 'God is our father' the primary meaning of our biological father is found to be unsuitable in the context and the meaning is then transferred. It seems that it is basically on account of the widespread acceptance of *lakṣaṇā* or the metaphorical mode, that the Thomist solution of the problem of the 'special sense that descriptive terms bear when they are applied to God' appeals to the Hindu mind.

In Hindu philosophy it is the schools which are centred directly on the Vedas, namely, those of Mīmāṁsā and Vedānta, that make the most use of *lakṣaṇā*. Although the 'theory of *lakṣaṇā* is important in all philosophical systems which try to discuss the nature of the ultimate Reality which is beyond expression',[9] the schools with a Vedic orientation tend to make special use of the following typology of *lakṣaṇā*: (a) where a part of the original meaning is preserved and a part rejected; (b) where the original meaning is preserved *in toto*; and (c) where the original meaning is altogether given up.

Let us now consider some statements in the Thomistic context and see how this analysis will apply to them.

Lakṣaṇā is described as of four kinds. In *jahallaksanā* the well-known meaning is put aside and a related one substituted. The stock example here is 'There is a hamlet on the Ganges.' Here the word Ganges really stands for the bank of the Ganges as no hamlet actually exists *on* the Ganges (no floating hamlets please). A Christian example would be a Biblical statement to the effect *God said*, when the expression is used by the reader at the pulpit, for it is the reader who is actually speaking and not God.

In *ajahallakṣaṇā* both the usual and related meanings are taken into account as in the stock example 'the lances are coming', wherein the word lance retains its usual meaning and also has the additional meaning of lance-bearers. To say *God is good* would belong here, for the usual meaning of goodness is retained as well as a sense of goodness known only to God is added.

In *jahadajahallakṣaṇā* part of the usual meaning is excluded and part is retained. The stock example here is: He is that John. Herein differences incidental and accidental to the identifications are left out, but the essential identity is asserted. *Jesus is the Saviour* would illustrate this form of *lakṣaṇā* in a Christian context. That Jesus was the son of Joseph is excluded, that he is the Saviour is retained.

The fourth type of *lakṣaṇā* is called *gauṇa vṛtti* and in it the meaning is apprehended not through the thing literally, but through its quality. The stock example here would be: Richard the lion-hearted. The meaning is grasped through the quality of courage, not literally. A Biblical example would be: *The Lord spake unto Joshua* for here 'it is not meant that God had a physical body with speech organs which set in motion sound waves which impinged on Joshua's eardrums', rather it is intended that God made his message so known to Joshua.

We can thus see how *lakṣaṇā* allows statements to be made to which the remarks made by K. Satchidananda Murty regarding the method of Aquinas also apply.

Since St. Thomas steers clear of the two pitfalls: (i) that of thinking that there is no reality which corresponds to the symbol we use, and (ii) that the unseen reality is *exactly* like the symbol; it seems to me that his view is fundamentally correct. Such a doctrine reminds us that while God is an inexpressible mystery which cannot be adequately expressed in our concepts and words, anthropomorphic symbolism is not a wholly unsuccessful endeavour to elucidate the content of revelation in which God has been apprehended as a loving and responding person.[10]

III

SPECIAL FEATURE OF HINDU THEOLOGICAL LANGUAGE IN RELATION TO GOD: THE CUMULATIVE APPROACH AS DISTINGUISHED FROM THE ANALOGICAL

Medieval Christian theology developed the doctrine of analogy in response to the basic question: how could one talk about God meaningfully, given the gulf that separates man and God?

Medieval Hindu theology also had to face the same problem. How could one, for instance, understand what God was, even if the scriptures told you so? It was pointed out earlier that there is one Upaniṣadic passage which is often cited in this context, and that it has been differently understood by the theistic and the absolutistic schools of Hindu thought. It will now be demonstrated that although the two schools derive different meanings from the same statement, the *procedure* adopted by them to arrive at their respective conclusions is identical.

The Upaniṣadic passage simply states that 'Brahman is reality, knowledge and infinity' (Taittirīyopaniṣad II.1: *satyam jñānam anantam brahma*).

In the absolutistic school of thought the statement is explained as follows. The first point to note is that, as they stand, the three terms *satya, jñāna* and *anantam* are adjectives of Brahman. But Śaṅkara argues that you can use adjectives to define things which belong to a class. Thus, for example, one can say 'blue lotus' and the adjective blue will serve to distinguish it from lotuses of different colors. This procedure works because 'this adjective negates the application of other adjectives. But there is no use applying adjectives to a unique thing' – which Brahman is –

'because there is no possibility of its being related to other adjectives at all.'[11] Śaṅkara, therefore, concludes that in these cases the adjectives are principally meant for definition and not as adjectives in the usual sense.

The next point to note is that the three terms, now taken definitionally rather than adjectivally, cumulatively generate the meaning of the statement. That is to say, each term tells us something about Brahman and the subsequent term corrects the error the preceding one might lead us into. Thus when it is said that Brahman is real (*satyam*) a doubt can arise as to whether, although it is real, the nature of its reality is material or spiritual. This is clarified by saying that Brahman is knowledge (*jñānam*): not only is Brahman real, but, we now know, it is a spiritual reality. Thus 'the word "knowledge" negates activity etc. and materiality. To remove the supposition that as knowledge is limited in the world, Brahman, which is knowledge is also limited, it is immediately added that Brahman is infinity'.[12]

Not only is the statement to be interpreted definitionally and cumulatively, it also has to be interpreted collectively, in that all the three descriptions apply to one Brahman. Vidyāraṇya, a scholar who belonged to the school of Śaṅkara, explains this point well by giving the illustration of verbally indicating the moon to someone. When the person is told 'the most shining one is the moon', the person identifies it. It should be noted that both 'the words shining and most are necessary; the former to exclude things such as the clouds and the latter to exclude the stars which shine but not so brightly'.[13] In the sentence from the Upaniṣad cited above, according to Vidyāraṇya 'the words reality, etc. have their own different general meanings, but as used here all of them have one impartite sense'.[14]

Thus it is clear that the Upaniṣadic statement is understood definitionally, cumulatively and collectively. Let us now examine the explication of the passage in the theistic school of Rāmānuja. Two points can be easily settled. First, the terms, 'real' and so on, are not used definitionally *the way Śaṅkara interprets them*, but adjectivally *and* definitionally, according to Rāmānuja as shown in an earlier chapter. Secondly, the expressions are not to be understood collectively as imparting an impartite sense because, in the school of Rāmānuja, Brahman possesses several auspicious qualities and those mentioned in the Upaniṣadic statement are some of them. One point now remains to be tackled – does Rāmānuja understand the terms cumulatively? This indeed seems to be the case, as was shown earlier. He uses *satyam* to exclude matter and souls involved in matter; *jñānam* to exclude released souls who were once bound; and *anantam* to exclude souls which were never bound. They do not share God's inherent infinity, for their infinity is that of attributive knowledge.

It is clear, therefore, that even though Śaṅkara and Rāmānuja differ in their metaphysical systems and in modes of conceptualising Brahman, both use what may be called *the cumulative method* to arrive at their results, which may be contrasted with the analogical method. The latter works vertically, the former horizontally.

Thus we have, I hope, identified one special Hindu way of talking of God – not merely discretely or aggregatively, but rather cumulatively. This view is further confirmed by the fact that modern Hindu scholars have used the same approach to explain another phrase by which Brahman is even more commonly described – namely, as *saccidānanda*:

> The spiritual and unitary character of this absolute reality is very well expressed by the classical phrase *saccidānanda*. As a single term defining its nature, it is met with only in the latter Upanishads; but its three elements – *sat*, *cit* and *ānanda* – are used of Brahman, singly and in pairs, even in the earliest of them. *Sat*, which means 'being,' points to the positive character of Brahman distinguishing it from all non-being. But positive entities, to judge from our experience, may be spiritual or not. The next epithet *cit*, which means 'sentience,' shows that it is spiritual. The last epithet *ānanda*, which stands for 'peace,' indicates its unitary and all-embracing character, in as much as variety is the source of all trouble and restlessness. 'Fear arises from the other,' as a famous Upanishadic saying has it. Thus the three epithets together signify that Brahman is the sole spiritual reality.[15]

The term is applied to Brahman by both the theistic and the absolutistic schools. The above illustration is absolutistic in nature. But it is easy to see how this approach may be extended to theism. Of the three expressions in *saccidānanda*, *sat*, *cit* and *ānanda*, the first two correspond to *satyam* and *jñānam* of the Upanishadic definition cited earlier. The earlier logic will apply here, with God to be distinguished from souls which were never bound, as being the abode of bliss with the ever-free souls deriving their bliss from communing with God.

IV

RELIGION AND LANGUAGE

Another view on religious language within Hinduism remains to be considered. In talking about religious language it has been assumed that religion and language are distinct phenomena and that there may be a particular kind of language called religious language. However an eminent Hindu thinker, Bhartṛhari (7th century AD) maintains that language is a religious phenomenon. This is in sharp and refreshing contrast to those who might be tempted to maintain that religion is a linguistic phenomenon – words full of sound and fury signifying nothing.

The argument is initially slightly technical, but should become simpler as we proceed. It also involves some assumptions basic to the Hindu religious tradition. One of them is the belief in the doctrine of the cyclical creation and dissolution of the universe. It should be noted that, at the beginning of each cycle, the text of the Veda flashes in the mind of Brahmā at the time of creation, implying that things are, in a sense, the manifestation of words. There is also the underlying assumption in much of Hindu linguistic theory that thought presupposes words mentally, just as objects presuppose words cosmologically.

Now the question Indian grammarians sought an answer to was this. The object the word denotes is a single entity, for example, a book – it has no temporal parts; but the word, when heard B-O-O-K, has temporal parts: how then can that which has parts generate an image which is impartite? Several answers were attempted, but the one we are concerned with is known as the doctrine of *sphoṭa*. According to this view words correspond to unitary symbols in our consciousness and what the word does is to manifest the *sphoṭa* or the symbol in consciousness. This is how words or sentences which are sequential generate meanings which are simultaneous, not time-bound.

From this viewpoint, then, the world of consciousness is full of innumerable *sphoṭas*. At this point the doctrine takes a religious turn. It was implied above that

> the existence of different *sphoṭas* is revealed by different words. It is important to remember, however, that according to the upholders of this theory, *sphoṭa* is ultimately *one* and not many; it is in fact the *only* Reality and identical with Brahman (*vide* Vākyapadīya). But like the Advaitins, these thinkers also admit that though reality is one from the transcendental point of view, it is many from the empirical or practical standpoint. They admit that though *sphoṭa* is ultimately one, it is not revealed in exactly the same form by every word, but that different forms or aspects of the *sphoṭa* are revealed by different words, just as different forms of the same face are revealed by different mirrors. There is, therefore, the phenomenal plurality of *sphoṭas* in spite of its noumenal unity.[16]

Actually in order to see the philosophical significance of this linguistic theory it might be a good idea to state Bhartṛhari's philosophical position now:

> To Bhartṛhari the linguistic theory of *sphoṭa* is part of his monistic and idealistic metaphysical theory according to which the transcendental speech-essence (*śabda-tattva*) is the First Principle of the universe. The *Vākyapadīya*, his monumental work on the philosophy of language, begins with the statement that the whole phenomenon of material existence is only an appearance (*vivarta*) of the speech principle which is identical with the ultimate Reality, Brahman. The entire world of things whose individuality consists only in names and forms (*nāma* and *rūpa*) has its source in this speech-essence. Symbol and meaning are only two aspects of the same principle. In fact it is the same speech-essence which appears in the form of various ideas or meanings on the one hand, and their symbols – words and sentences – on the other hand, and thus constitutes the entire phenomenal world. This speech-essence, which is the ultimate Reality and is of the nature of consciousness, has neither beginning nor end and is unchanging; but on the basis of its various powers such as Time, which, though in essence identical with it, seem to be different, the phenomenal world appears as evolutionary and pluralistic. The *śabda-tattva* is not limited by time; the eternal timeless appears as changing owing to the working of the time factor. Time is an inherent power of the Absolute and exerts its influence in bringing about the powers of *śabda-tattva*.[17]

Another school which gave a quasi-religious significance to language was the Mīmāṁsā school of Vedānta which, beginning with the eternality of the letters, built up a theory of the eternality of the Vedas. The theory now is largely of historical rather than philosophical interest.[18]

The Mīmāṁsakas were atheistic and Bhartṛhari is monistic, while the main emphasis of the current study is theistic. It should therefore not be overlooked that language does play an important role in Hindu theism. According to Rāmānuja, for instance, 'all words, directly or indirectly, refer to brahman'.[19]

> Every word eventually signifies the supreme God, as everything eventually points to him as the final essence. Hence language is richer in content for a knower than it is for the ordinary man. All words are signs to remind the wise man of God, as all objects are for him windows through which to see God.[20]

V

THE LIMITS OF LANGUAGE AND THE LIMITS OF RELIGIOUS EXPERIENCE

A modern Hindu thinker K. Satchidananda Murty has some stimulating thoughts to offer on the question of language. He points out, first, that 'theology has not yet developed a language fully appropriate to deal with the personal encounter between man and God'. This does not surprise him for 'it is only within the last two centuries that science has (as James Jeans says) constructed its own language or jargon as some may prefer to call it', and 'theology has had to deal with 'things' which are more concrete and complex than scientific things'.[21] Secondly, drawing next on Eddington rather than James Jeans, he points out that 'the vocabulary of scientific intercourse has had a far-reaching effect on the development of science, leading us to the conclusion that the limit to scientific observation is the limit of our logical vocabulary'. He goes on to say: 'It follows from this that the foundation of Quantum theory (e.g.) is linguistic, and that Heisenberg's principle is a consequence of the atomicity of scientific language'.[22]

Perhaps it is best to conclude by differing from the conclusions in some ways, while recognising their challenging nature. The religious traditions of mankind have had a fairly long run to evolve their vocabulary and should have done better than science, unless we take the new situation created by the emergence of the 'global village' into account. Then it is of course true that the cross-cultural philosophy of religion has not yet evolved its own language with the same precision and clarity that science has. On the other question of logical vocabulary setting the limit to scientific observation, it is also evidently true that, unless one can articulate the observation, in a sense it remains unobserved. But the observation can also inspire the observer to its proper articulation, as seems to have been the case in the past when new terms have been coined in science. It may be true that in the *textual study* of religion the ultimate philosophical points might turn on those of grammar, whether it be the Bible or the Veda. But the philosophy of religion must always ask the question M. Hiriyanna raises when discussing the philosophy of Rāmānuja. He explains Rāmānuja's basic categories with the example of a blue lotus. 'A blue lotus is a unity in the sense that the material substance of the flower, which is characterized by two qualities that are different from it as well as from each other, viz. "blueness" and "lotusness" is one'. This serves to illustrate the point that Brahman is a unity as encompassing matter and souls, but matter and souls are different from each other and from Brahman – though all are inseparable. Then he goes on to say:

> There is no doubt that Rāmānuja has here hit upon a very plausible way of interpreting co-ordinate propositions, and has thereby successfully got over the difficulty which the Upanishads present. Where they distinguish the world or the self from Brahman, they give expression to what is a matter of fact. Where they identify them, they only mean that they are inseparable in the sense explained just now, and not that they are identical. It may be doubted whether it is altogether sound to draw a metaphysical conclusion from forms of linguistic usage – to take 'the grammar of language for the grammar of reality'.[23]

Indeed one might conclude a chapter on religious language with the question of how the grammar of language and the grammar of reality are related to each other.

Notes and References

1. M. Hiriyanna, *The Essentials of Indian Philosophy* (London: George Allen & Unwin, 1949) p. 102.
2. S. M. Srinivasa Chari, *Advaita and Viśiṣṭādvaita* (Delhi: Motilal Banarsidass, 1976) pp. 80–1.
3. See K. Satchidananda Murty, *Revelation and Reason in Advaita Vedānta* (New York: Columbia University Press, 1959) ch. IV.
4. Ibid., p. 286.
5. Ibid., pp. 289–90.
6. K. Kunjunni Raja, *Indian Theories of Meaning* (Wheaton, Illinois: Adyar Library and Research Center, 1969) ch. 6. *Upamāna* does not seem to apply here (ibid., p. 30).
7. Ibid., pp. 241–2.
8. See John H. Hick, *Philosophy of Religion*, 3rd edn (Englewood Cliffs, New Jersey: Prentice-Hall, 1983) pp. 77–9.
9. K. Kunjunni Raja, op. cit., p. 253.
10. K. Satchidananda Murty, op. cit., p. 290.
11. Ibid.
12. Ibid.
13. Ibid., pp. 65–6.
14. Ibid., p. 66.
15. M. Hiriyanna, op. cit., p. 22.
16. D. M. Datta, *The Six Ways of Knowing* (University of Calcutta, 1972) p. 258, fn. 1.
17. K. Kunjunni Raja, op. cit., pp. 146–7.
18. For a brief account see M. Hiriyanna, *Outlines of Indian Philosophy* (London: George Allen & Unwin, 1964 [first published 1932]), pp. 307–13.
19. S. Radhakrishnan, *Indian Philosophy*, vol. II (London: George Allen & Unwin, 1927) p. 688.
20. M. Hiriyanna, *The Essentials of Indian Philosophy* p. 184.
21. K. Satchidananda Murty, op. cit., p. 291.
22. Ibid.
23. M. Hiriyanna, *Essentials*, pp. 178–9. A slightly more telling if technical example may be added from Haridas Bhattacharyya (ed.), *The Cultural Heritage of India*, vol. III (Calcutta: Ramakrishna Mission Institute of Culture, 1953 [first published 1937]) p. 490: 'Vātsyāyana, for example, inquires how the self as Ātman, that must be accepted as the logical presupposition of the process of proof, can itself be turned into an object of proof, how the *pramātr* may be taken to be a *prameya*. Apparently, the question is insoluble within the postulates of the Nyāya philosophy; and it must either be admitted that the process of proving implies the existence of the prover just as doubt implies the existence of the doubter, as Descartes said, or that every attempt to know the knower would inevitably lead to argument in a circle, as was seen by Kant. But Vātsyāyana, instead of following any of these courses, seeks to cut the Gordian knot by taking recourse to the case-endings of Sanskrit grammar, according to which the same thing

may be regarded as being the subject of a sentence or its predicate depending upon the intention of the verb. A tree, for example, may be used in a sentence either as a nominative or as an accusative; this is supposed by Vātsyayāna to be a sufficient guarantee for the assertion that the self too may be the agent as well as the object of proof, the *kartṛ* as well as the *karma*. The appeal to the grammatical structure of a language for solving a philosophical issue has not perhaps assumed a more irrational form than what is illustrated here. The syntactical rules governing the construction of sentences cannot be brought in for the solution of an epistemological issue, and Vātsyāyana does not appear to see the ambiguity in the terms *kartṛ* and *karma* when they are used in sentence-construction on the one hand, and in the analysis of knowledge on the other.'

6

The Problem of Falsification and Verification

The discussion of religious language in the previous chapters indicated a difference of opinion regarding its function: is the function of religious language to make factual assertions or does it perform a non-cognitive function? The chief views held in relation to religious language as essentially non-cognitive in nature were also surveyed. It needs to be recognised now that:

> In implicit opposition to all noncognitive accounts of religious language, traditional Christian and Jewish faith has always presumed the factual character of its basic assertions. It is, of course, evident even to the most preliminary reflection that theological statements, having a unique subject matter, are not wholly like any other kind of statement. They constitute a special use of language, which it is the task of the philosophy of religion to examine. However, the way in which this language operates within historic Judaism and Christianity is much closer to ordinary factual asserting than to either the expressing of aesthetic intuitions or the declaring of ethical policies.[1]

In view of this 'deeply ingrained tendency of traditional theism to use the language of fact',[2] we must now examine the claim of religion, via religious language, to the making of factual assertions more closely.

A factual claim, by definition, consists of a proposition which declares a certain state of affairs to be true or otherwise. Now the question which naturally arises in respect to these claims is: how do we know that they are true? It will be useful to note here that all verifiable claims are factual but all factual claims are not necessarily verifiable. The claim that angels exist is factual but not, in the usual sense of the term, verifiable. On what grounds, then, is one to accept statements which claim to be factual but are not verifiable?

I

The standard approach within a religious tradition has been to appeal to the authority of the scripture of that tradition; that is, to revelation. Such a claim may be acceptable in theology, but in the philosophy of religion we must now ask: on what grounds should the authority of the sacred scriptures be accepted? The answer given in Christianity and in the Nyāya school of Hinduism is: because it is the word of God.

Such a position is open to serious criticism from a philosophical point of view, which has been articulated forcefully by Hobbes. His criticism may be summarised thus:

> We have not heard God speaking to us; if we believe the Bible to be God's Word, we are really believing the person or the tradition (the Church) saying so, rather than God, because we have not ourselves seen him revealing what is in the Bible. So, in this case, what we believe is that person or tradition, not God himself; and if we disbelieve the Bible to be God's word, we are disbelieving that person or institution, and not disbelieving God. Hobbes gives examples to make this clear: If Livy wrote that the gods once made a cow speak, and if I do not believe it, what I distrust thereby is Livy and not the gods. If a historian writes that Julius Caesar fought alone against a battalion and won, and if I do not believe it, it is that historian whom I do not believe, and not Caesar. Hobbes concludes that if anyone claims that God has spoken to him, and if another cannot believe him, no argument of the former can convince the latter.[3]

The argument, though couched here in terms of the Bible, also applies to the Vedas with equal force, if they are regarded as the word of God, as in Nyāya.[4]

An alternative line of reasoning could be urged, that the scriptures are valid because they constitute the testimony of capable and trustworthy witnesses. Such an argument is in fact used in Hinduism and could easily be extended to Christianity.[5] This argument seems to possess more force than the previous one, but is still open to what, from a philosophical point of view, would be perhaps a fatal objection, namely, that excellence of character and competence is no guarantee of truth, however much it may enhance the probability of it being so. Indeed we can take two positions here which basically reflect the same attitude: (a) the statement is independent of the person who makes it; it is *what* is said regarding which truth or falsehood has to be determined and not *who* said it;[6] or (b) 'The criterion for truth or falsehood of a statement is independent of the statement itself; and is its "truth-content", which is nothing else than reality.'[7] Indeed:

> The utmost that could be proved about a religious scripture is that its author or authors were not impostors; but it can never be *proved* that its teaching is true, in the sense in which a scientific proposition is proved true. If we have reasons for believing that a religious book was written by an *āpta* [i.e. one who has direct experience of what he speaks about, who desires to communicate what he experiences only, and who is able to do so] then it can only lead us to conclude that what he says was absolute truth for himself, and not that it is a verifiable universal truth for all men. Since every scripture (even if it is not spurious) is just a pattern of words, – first orally handed down, then written and then printed – meant to be a vehicle of revelation, to regard it as a collection of infallible oracles dropped down from heaven (as the Cabbalists, the Muslims, the Hindus and some Christians believe) is to develop a religion of the Book and not a religion of the Spirit,[8] or one based on Reason.[9]

Another variation of the argument just criticised has been advanced: 'that since the ethical insights of the prophets and sages, whose teachings are contained in religious scriptures are recognized to be true, what they say about God must also be true'.[10] It is easily seen that the latter need not necessarily follow from the former; they could be right in the former respect but not in the latter. The point has an important application to Hinduism. The Vedas are regarded as authoritative solely in respect to both (a) *dharma* or morality and (b) *mokṣa* or salvation. The point does not seem to have been debated within the tradition that it may be authoritative only with respect to *one* of the two.

One more point could be raised. Scriptural statements could be defended by claiming on their behalf what is claimed of scientific statements, namely, that they are verifiable. This point will emerge again later, but at this stage let it merely be asked: 'how can one verify scriptural sentences?' At least one response to the question has been thus criticised.

> Some Christian Protestant thinkers (e.g.) say that the excellence of the Bible provides its own inward evidence, meaning thereby that since it produces an 'impact' on the reader, which is unique, it must be true. But this is a dangerous argument, because many tales (e.g., the stories of King Arthur), dramas (e.g., *Hamlet*), and novels (e.g., *The Brothers Karamazov*) have exerted a tremendous influence on the emotions and actions of men; and yet, they are false.[11]

Although the argument that scriptural statements are verifiable in the sense claimed above fails to convince, it provides the context for a more detailed discussion of what is involved in the verifiability of statements.

II

John Hick identifies the position on the question of verifiability as applied to religious propositions thus: 'The basic principle – representing a modified version of the original verifiability principle of the logical positivists – [is that] a factual assertion is one whose truth or falsity makes an experienceable difference'.[12] Two basic elements are involved in this approach: one of them is the possibility of establishing the truth or falsity of an assertion. The other is that the truth or falsity 'must make some experienceable difference.' The distinction is important and will have to be pressed into service later. But what is meant by saying that the truth or falsity should make an experienceable difference? Hick explains:

> Suppose, for example, the startling news is announced one morning that overnight the entire physical universe has instantaneously doubled in size and that the speed of light has doubled. At first, this news seems to point to a momentous scientific discovery. All the items composing the universe, including our own bodies, are now twice as big as they were yesterday. But inevitable questions concerning the evidence for

> this report must be raised. How can anyone know that the universe has doubled in size? What observable difference does it make whether this is so or not; what events or appearances are supposed to reveal it? On further reflection, it becomes clear that there *could not* be any evidence for this particular proposition, for if the entire universe has doubled and the speed of light has doubled with it, our measurements have also doubled and we can never know that any change has taken place. If our measuring rod has expanded with the objects to be measured, it cannot measure their expansion. In order adequately to acknowledge the systematic impossibility of testing such a proposition, it seems best to classify it as (cognitively) meaningless. It first seemed to be a genuinely factual assertion, but under scrutiny it proves to lack the basic characteristic of an assertion, namely, that it must make an experienceable difference whether the facts are as alleged or not.[13]

Two scholars of Hindu thought have argued that religious statements are capable of being verified. One of them maintains that they can be verified in terms of truth and falsity, while the other maintains that they can make an experienceable difference. We shall examine the representative of the second view first.

Pratima Bowes raises the question of truth and falsity, interestingly enough, in the context of Hindu polytheism, and asks: 'in what sense is polytheism (or anything else) true? Are there really divinities called Indra, Agni, etc., who have power to confer gifts on men?' 'Now it seems to me obvious', she goes on to say, 'that propositions of a religious nature which are apparently descriptive (saying that God or a god is such and such) are not descriptive in the straightforward sense which allows verification by means of correspondence.'[14] In what sense, then, are they true?

To answer this question Bowes develops the concept of an archetype, a concept which should not be confused with Jungian or Eliadean archetypes, homonymy notwithstanding. Following Max Black, by an archetype Bowes means 'a systematic repertoire of ideas by means of which a given thinker describes, *by analogical extension*, some domain to which these ideas do not immediately and literally apply'.[15] Bowes indicates that such a concept of archetypes can be usefully applied to the religious field in two ways. One of these is intellectual, in that it enables us to 'talk about the field of religious reality, which will remain inaccessible otherwise'.[16] The one which concerns us here, however, is the second – its pragmatic use.

> By organising our thoughts, emotions, etc., in a determinate way these archetypes enable us to pursue a definite course of discipline or religious practice whereby we can positively link ourselves with religious reality. And this is what religion is ultimately all about; so although verification by correspondence is not available, some kind of validation by pragmatic test is. And this means that if the use of an archetype enables us to find religious reality and integrate ourselves with it then it is valid or true in this field. In order to do this, of course, an archetype must be such as to be capable of unveiling, to some degree, the mystery of religious reality.[17]

Bowes argues that although 'archetypes are not true in a literal descriptive sense' as 'there are not literally speaking beings called "gods" who reside in heaven or wherever', yet 'we can see the powers that affect us as gods if this helps us to integrate ourselves with life and with religious reality'.[18]

This approach invites an immediate criticism. If we are going to decide the verity or otherwise of religious statements in terms of their pragmatic value, then have we not already abandoned the question of truth-value which started us on the quest for verification in the first place? This argument has considerable force but the Hindu response to it is interesting, for two reasons. First, the point is obvious to the Hindu thinker too that the frame of reference has been changed. Then why does the Hindu philosopher persist in using the language of truth when one would expect the philosopher to employ utilitarian language? The Hindu answer is not without interest even if it may not be entirely convincing in a positivist way. It may be summarised thus: Religious reality, whether theistic or absolutistic, is characterised by infinity. This means that it 'is free of the spatio-temporal limitations of finitude'.[19] We, as human beings, however, are subject to such finitude so that any statement made about the religious reality characterised by infinity is bound to fall short. Therefore it is not possible to expect verity or otherwise in relation to statements about God. They can never be fully true because God is infinite, but they can never be fully false in the sense that our own existence is grounded in that very reality. Therefore the only sensible way one may speak of religious statements as true or false is in terms not of their truth-value but their value, for their truth is contained in their value.

The second reason follows from the first. The religious reality, being infinite, cannot be described in terms of finitude; but although that reality cannot be fully described, it can be experienced. One could at this point raise the interesting question – can an infinite reality ever be even fully experienced? Opinions differ on this,[20] but there is general agreement that religious reality can be experienced, even if one is not quite certain whether it can be exhaustively experienced. Such experience constitutes verification. Therefore the truth-value of a statement about religious reality must lie in its ability to lead to the realisation of the truth it claims to represent. Even if such an approach is accepted, however, the verification principle can be pressed further: how do we know the alleged experience is genuine or spurious? This properly calls for a separate study, but it should suffice to point out here that not only the Hindu but all the ancient religious traditions of India recognise and address the problem, and have even tried to devise ways of sifting genuine from spurious experiences. Even such a popular text as the Bhagavadgītā repeatedly discusses the signs which characterise a realised person.[21]

The other approach which can be related to the verification principle has been developed by Karl H. Potter in the context of Hindu philosophy. He develops his approach in full awareness of the contemporary philosophical situation in respect of the positivist emphasis on verification and hopes that what he says 'may have some interest for contemporary philosophers independently of any value it may have for the exposition of Indian thought, for it addresses a problem currently under heavy discussion, namely, the question whether moral reasoning is or is not to be conceived analogously to reasoning about matters of fact'.[22]

Potter begins by making a key distinction when he suggests that the verification principle may be discussed in two distinct contexts: (a) in ascertaining the claims of a value, such as *mokṣa* or freedom in the Hindu context or (b) 'in discovering what we ought to do in order to realise an ultimate value already discovered', that is, determined.[23]

He restricts his exposition to the second situation, one in which the value is already known or 'given'. Next Potter develops the concept of a challenge and defines challenge as 'a felt tension in a situation',[24] the expression 'felt' being intended to convey a conscious recognition of it as opposed to an unconscious tension.[25] This tension arises in a situation of 'disparity between one's capacities' and 'one's performance or expected performance'.[26] Once a challenge is experienced one may decide to react to it or to let it pass. Once it is assessed as 'an appropriate challenge'[27] the concept of 'role' becomes important, for it is in this context that Potter introduces the concept of verification, namely, as the verification of a role. Potter points out that such verification can only be thought of further in the context of an appropriate challenge.

> Verification of roles is another thing. Just as it makes little sense to deliberate about the truth or falsity of meaningless noises, so it makes little sense to experiment with challenges recognized as inappropriate. But once a challenge is thought to be appropriate (granting that one may still be wrong about this), the next thing the seeker for freedom wishes to discover is whether responding to it will in fact lead him toward his desired goal, complete freedom, along a path of increasing control.[28]

Now the analogy with the scientific process of verification is developed. If the person makes the judgement that 'meeting the challenge will lead to greater control' – that is to say, the challenge is an appropriate challenge, then he has just made a 'prediction' which is capable of being verified. Now two courses are open: 'One can either commit himself overtly to the challenge with whatever consequences its falsification may entail, or one may experiment in the imagination.'[29] The first course of action is obvious,[30] the second is explained thus: 'In verifying or falsifying a role, we use our imagination to construct the role and then judge whether the fulfilment of the role will lead to greater control. If when carefully considered it appears to do so, the role is verified; if not, it is falsified.'[31]

Even if one were to go along thus far one might baulk at this last step as too subjective, for, while scientists actually verify or falsify hypotheses, Potter takes verification or falsification to mean *either* 'the actual confrontation of a role with certain concrete actions in fulfilment of the role, *or* rehearsal of such confrontation in one's mind [my italic]'.[32] 'Thus it might appear', remarks Potter, 'that I will count an apparent verification or falsification as a real one, where the scientist insists on an actual confrontation'.[33] But he goes on to say:

> In fact, however, I don't think the scientist insists on an actual confrontation in most cases. My inquiring man might, after all, insist on a crucial experiment in every case before he satisfied himself that his role was verified, but he knows that in practical affairs he cannot wait upon such developments; that is why he introspects and tries to imagine what would happen if he adopted a certain role. The scientist, too, must judge concerning the verification or falsification of many hypotheses without waiting for a crucial experiment. Crucial experiments are the exception rather than the rule. What the scientist typically does is to reason back from what would be the case if thus and so should occur until he finds a necessary condition for it which contradicts something highly verified already; then he concludes that his hypothesis won't do. Direct confrontation is very hard, and only in a few celebrated cases has it been possible. Indirect verification, which is the normal kind, consists in being satisfied after enough reasoning coupled with enough testing that no contradiction with established facts can be found. It is then a matter of words whether you want to call the more normal procedure 'verification' or only 'apparent verification'; in any case, it's all that one is likely to be able to achieve except in the unusual case.[34]

We have now considered two suggestions of what might be called the Hindu version of scientific verification and falsification. Both of these approaches are deeply rooted in the Hindu worldview, one metaphysically, the other psychologically. Both also accept certain Hindu presuppositions: that there are 'many truths' or that freedom (*mokṣa*) is the goal of life, although it is possible to detach the views themselves analytically from the Hindu setting. These views no doubt serve to articulate the Hindu position plausibly in a modern idiom, but the conclusion is difficult to avoid that the rules of the game of the Western philosophy of religion have not been observed. Bowes seems to sidetrack the truth issue and Potter that of objective verifiability. Where these approaches do help is in introducing an experiential dimension to the issue. It is here that they perhaps raise a point of some interest for the Western philosophy of religion. Does the difference that results in a person's life as visualised under these approaches qualify as an 'experienceable difference'? And if it does, then do we still need two criteria to accept a proposition as true? For in effect what Bowes and Potter could be seen as suggesting is that a proposition should be accepted as true if it makes an 'experienceable difference' to a person's life.

This would represent a new kind of solution to the problem created by the application of 'the verifiability principle of the logical positivists – that a factual assertion is one whose truth or falsity makes some experienceable difference' to 'teleological propositions'. It would imply either that 'experienceable difference' by itself should be a criterion, and perhaps even the criterion of truth. Or more daringly that 'the experienceable difference' be no longer related to the question of truth or falsity. This comes dangerously close to the position that if God did not exist we would have to invent him/her, except that from this viewpoint there is a religious reality and God is a way we have invented to refer to it.

III

We may now turn to an examination of the problems created for traditional theism by the application of the verification principle to theological propositions in more detail.

One such attempt has been made by John Wisdom whose parable of the gardener has often been referred to.[35] According to this parable 'two people return to their long-neglected garden' and find that it shows signs of being maintained but no gardener is to be seen. From this state of affairs one concludes that 'a gardener comes' and the other that he doesn't. Now Wisdom argues that when, even after a careful examination of the situation, one of them believes that a gardener comes and the other that he does not, then 'their different words now reflect no difference as to what they have found in the garden, no difference as to what they would find in the garden if they looked further and no difference about how fast unattended gardens fall into disorder'.[36] Thus the statement whether there is a gardener or not is no longer a question of fact, but reflects ways of looking at the same set of facts. If the word God is substituted for gardener the significance of the parable in the context of theism becomes clear. Thus theists and atheists 'are not making mutually contradictory assertions but are expressing different feelings . . . we can no longer say in any usual sense that one is right and the other is wrong'.[37] This leads to a position rather similar to one developed earlier under the influence of Hindu thought, for John H. Hick goes on to remark that we would now have to speak of 'these different feelings as being more or less satisfying or valuable: as Santayana said, religions are not true or false but better or worse'.[38] There is the further point that 'there is no disagreement about experienceable facts, the settlement of which would determine whether the theist or the atheist is right'.[39] No verification is possible if edification is.

Here some comments suggest themselves from a Hindu point of view. The parable in effect suggests that there is no valid means of knowing whether the gardener exists or not. Perception (*pratyakṣa*) fails because the gardener is not seen. Inference (*anumāna*) fails because the two people draw opposite inferences. Analogy or comparison (*upamāna*) fails because to say 'the gardener is like God' will not work because the gardener's own existence is in doubt and so is God's. Now what would work in Hindu thought would be a statement based on dependable verbal authority from someone *else* who has seen the gardener or knows for certain that there is a gardener. But no such dependable source is around. Thus a very general application of the Hindu epistemological categories of Nӯaya shows that existence of the gardener is not predicable.

At this point then we must recognise that there is some 'factor' in operation which accounts for the condition of the garden as it is. Although we cannot decide *what* it is, we cannot deny *that* it is. Here Hinduism, taking its stand on religious reality rather than God, and in postulating various different forms of relationship between the world and God, provides more room for accommodation.

A good historical illustration of the point of the parable of the gardener is provided by the earthquake which devastated a large part of the Indian province of Bihar on 15 January 1934.[40] Two major figures of modern India – Gandhi and Tagore – took opposite stands on it in relation to theism. Gandhi 'visited the stricken area in March; he walked barefoot from village to village, comforting, teaching, and preaching'.[41] But he also told the surviving victims, and the rest of the world, that it was the sin of untouchability which had 'brought down God's vengeance upon certain parts of Bihar'.[42] He saw God's hand in the disaster, it was 'a chastisement for your sins', mainly 'the sin of untouchability'.[43] Rabindranath Tagore, who was no atheist, chose to view the event as a purely natural phenomenon and issued a statement criticising Gandhi. Gandhi held his ground, claiming that for him 'connection between cosmic phenomena and human behaviour is a living faith and draws me nearer to God'.[44] It is clear that the point cannot be settled by an appeal to the facts of the earthquake: it has become a matter of interpretation, and, what is more, a matter of difference of opinion among two theists.

Just as John Wisdom applied the concept of verifiability to theological propositions, Anthony Flew applies the concept of falsification to these propositions. He asks the following penetrating question in relation to God:

> What would have to occur or to have occurred to constitute for you a disproof of the love of, or of the existence of, God?[45]

It is clear that nothing could conceivably falsify the existence of God. For one could always fall back on God's inscrutability, the doctrine of *deus absconditus* which 'according to Max Weber constitutes the only consistent theodicy the Western world has to offer'.[46]

One must here distinguish, as Flew does not seem to, between two issues: (a) the existence of God and (b) the love of God. For philosophically God can exist without having to be loving. There is a further distinction to be drawn between God and some impersonal force which may underlie the universe. There are, for instance, those who have concluded that God may exist but is not necessarily loving, or that God does not exist but some impersonal force does. Three musings of the famous Hindi novelist, Premchand (d. 1936) serve to illustrate the point. In one of his novels (*Kāyākalpa*) he shows his preoccupation with the question of reconciling God with the existence of an unjust world. 'Interspersed throughout the novel are such musings as these: 'Why did God create a world, where there is so much selfishness, envy and injustice? Was it not possible to create a world where all men, all communities could live with peace and happiness? What sort of justice is this that one revels in luxury and another is pushed around; one nation sucks the blood of another and lords over it, while the other starves and is crushed under foot?' Such an unjust world cannot have been created by God.'[47] Then he writes in a letter to a friend: 'I had formerly believed in a force above all. Not as a conclusion based on thinking, but only as a traditional belief. That faith is now shattered. Undoubtedly there is some great power behind the universe. But I cannot believe that it has anything to do with human affairs, just as it cannot have anything to do with the affairs of ants, flies or mosquitoes.'[48] And finally, when a friend raised the question of God when Premchand was close to death he replied: 'Your God is a God of wrath and punishment, and runs the world by the rod. I shall never worship a God who behaves in this ridiculously inhuman fashion. God may be kind to the rich, for they seem to have all the comforts; but He isn't very kind to us common folk. I cannot believe in God as long as I see cruelty and injustice in the world. I don't have faith in absolute values. If I find that by telling a lie, I can save the lives of thousands of people or bring them positive benefit in any other way, I'll lie gladly. I measure an action by its value to human beings. If it helps my fellow beings, anything I do is good; if it harms them, it is evil.'[49]

It is the task of philosophy as much to clarify questions as to attempt to answer them. In the musings of Premchand, for instance, the following points need to be disentangled: (a) the existence of a *benevolent* God is not consistent with injustice: (b) God as a personal God may be indifferent to human suffering; (c) there may be no God but an impersonal force which is indifferent to suffering; (d) one should adopt a utilitarian attitude towards ethics.

It is interesting to use Premchand here because he does not bring Karma into the discussion at all and thus we find his position close to Flew's. What Flew has done is to show that 'the Judaic-Christian belief in a loving God' is not falsifiable; not that belief in God is not falsifiable. It may be that belief in God is not falsifiable as well, but in the Hindu context one would have to follow a different route because of the doctrine of karma which can be used to insulate God from the problem of evil. One could also then, of course, maintain, that the doctrine of karma, like the love of God, is not falsifiable.

There is however one point which is worth considering here within the context of Hindu philosophy which may have some bearing on the falsifiability thesis – though only indirectly. I would now like to argue that the existence of God though not *empirically falsifiable*, may be *philosophically verifiable*. Let us consider the Hindu system of philosophy known as Advaita Vedānta. This system of philosophy regards the Impersonal Absolute as the ultimate reality. This Impersonal Absolute is called Brahman – *nirguṇa brahman* – the sole spiritual reality free from distinctions of any kind. In relation to it the visible plurality of the universe is explained as the product of *māyā*. It will be easily seen that the system can thus function quite effectively *without invoking God*. This is clearly implied by such statements that *saguṇa* or 'qualified Brahman, *if personified*, becomes the God or Īśvara of Advaita [my italics]'.[50] Eliot Deutsch is more explicit:

> Theoretically, it would seem that the doctrine of *māyā* as a 'concealing' and 'distorting' power can account for Appearance, as far as it can be accounted for, without the need for Īśvara as an explanatory concept; and especially since it is maintained that the 'existence' of Īśvara as such cannot be demonstrated rationally. Īśvara, according to Advaita Vedānta, can be affirmed only on the grounds of experience, as a content of experience (as *saguṇa* Brahman, the harmonization of distinctions), or as a necessary condition for spiritual experience.[51]

If God is not an 'explanatory concept' and is not required by the logic of the system, then what is it doing there? It could, of course, be regarded as a concession to popular taste,[52] but if the system is seen as possessing philosophical integrity then the point cannot be dismissed so easily. Philosophical verifiability suggests the point that when a proposition is found in a philosophical system which can otherwise function smoothly without it, and no obvious historical, sociological or non-philosophical explanation adequately explains its presence then the proposition may be regarded as *philosophically* verified in the absence of any other valid explanation now remaining apart from its truth.

IV

We saw earlier how the principle of verification was introduced in the philosophy of religion through the issue of the nature of religious language. Once introduced, the principle of verification, along with that of falsification, was applied to theological propositions and the conclusion was drawn that theological propositions such as that of the existence of God are neither verifiable nor falsifiable. It was even hinted that perhaps they are not meant to be so, an idea which takes us back in part to the non-cognitive theories of religious language. Three solutions to this dilemma of the verifiability/falsifiability of theological propositions have been suggested and they may now be examined.

One such solution is associated with the name of R. M. Hare, who has introduced the notion of a *blik*. A *blik* is defined as 'being an unverifiable and unfalsifiable interpretation of one's experience'.[53] The concept is illustrated with the help of the example of a lunatic who is convinced that all the professors want to kill him. If he is sufficiently convinced of the murderous intent of all professors then it would be impossible to persuade him to the contrary, for any such effort will be seen by him as further proof of the felonious deviousness of the professors. Hare distinguishes this insane *blik* of the lunatic from our sane *blik* in relation to professors.

The point then is that with certain propositions it is not their truth or falsity which is important but, as in this case, their sanity or insanity. The fact that some propositions are not verifiable or falsifiable does not carry the implication that therefore they need not be held at all and that holding or not holding them makes no difference. For instance, it is not verifiable or falsifiable to hold that everything happens by chance, a doctrine known as *yadṛcchāvāda*[54] in ancient India. But

> suppose we believe that everything that happened, happened by pure chance. This would not of course be an assertion; for it is compatible with anything happening or not happening, and so, incidentally, is its contradictory. But if we had this belief, we should not be able to explain or predict or plan anything. Thus, although we should not be *asserting* anything different from those of a more normal belief, there would be a great difference between us; and this is the sort of difference that there is between those who really believe in God and those who really disbelieve in him.[55]

A few points need to be noticed regarding the concept of *blik*. 'Hare abandons as indefensible the traditional view of religious statements as being or entertaining assertions that are true or false.'[56] To that extent he agrees with those who say that religious statements are non-cognitive but he goes further and says that one could still distinguish between sane and insane *bliks*. He is criticised for this by Hick who says:

> We want to distinguish, in Hare's terminology, between right and wrong *bliks*. In the previously quoted passage, Hare as-

> sumes that one can make this distinction, for he identifies one *blik* as sane and the contrary *blik* as insane. However, there seems to be an inconsistency in his position here, for a discrimination between sane (= right) and insane (= wrong) *bliks* is ruled out by his insistence that *bliks* are unverifiable and unfalsifiable. If experience can never yield either confirmation or disconfirmation of *bliks*, there is no basis for speaking of them as being right or wrong, appropriate or inappropriate, sane or insane. These distinctions make sense only if it also makes sense to refer to tests, evidence, and verification.[57]

It is possible, it seems, to defend Hare against Hick here by drawing some distinctions and by employing some Hindu philosophical ideas. Three sets of dichotomies have been used interchangeably, as it were, in the foregoing discussion: the distinction between *false* and *true*, between *right* and *wrong* and between *sane* and *insane*. By using them loosely, the fact is lost sight of that the criterion for distinguishing one member of the pair from another changes as we use one pair rather than another. The distinction between truth and falsity, in this case, is an empirical judgement. The distinction between right and wrong involved a moral judgement. The distinction between sanity and insanity is a psychological judgement. It is not true to say that 'there is no basis' for speaking of *bliks* as 'being right or wrong, appropriate or inappropriate, sane or insane'.[58] It is true that it is not the *same* basis as the one used for distinguishing true from false, but to say that there is no basis *at all* seems to be an overstatement. Maybe there will be no complete agreement on a criterion but this is again different from implying that there are no possible criteria for making such a distinction. In fact Hick himself suggests a criterion without realising it, when he says: 'Probably everyone would agree that, when sincerely held, religious beliefs make an important difference *to the believer*'.[59] For the effect of the belief on the believer can itself serve as a criterion of the appropriateness or otherwise of a *blik*. This is a standard Hindu position which has found expression here in quasi-modern terminology.[60] But the criticism against Hare's position, that it does not allow verifiability and falsifiability in the positivist sense to be applied to theological statement, seems to be sound.

The second solution to the problem has been suggested by Basil Mitchell, who

> recounts his own parable. A member of the resistance movement in an occupied country meets a stranger who deeply impresses him as being truthful and trustworthy and who claims to be the resistance leader. He urges the partisan to have faith in him whatever may happen. Sometimes the stranger is seen apparently aiding the resistance and sometimes apparently collaborating with the enemy. Nevertheless the partisan continues in trust. He admits that on the face of it some of the stranger's actions strain this trust. However, he has faith, even though at times his faith is sorely tried, that there is a satisfactory explanation of the stranger's ambiguous behavior.[61]

As Hick has pointed out, in contrast to the earlier solution suggested by Hare,

> Mitchell's parable is concerned with a straight-forward matter of fact which can, in principle, be definitely ascertained. The stranger himself knows on which side he is, and after the war, when all the facts are brought to light, the ambiguity of his behavior will be resolved and his true character made clear. Thus, Mitchell is concerned with stressing the similarity rather than the dissimilarity between religious beliefs and ordinary, unproblematic factual beliefs.[62]

The stranger in the parable is, of course, God. Perhaps there is the further implication that he has made himself known to us through his word so that, even though our experience in this world may apparently be in conflict with and contradict what he has told us about himself, or we have been told about him for that matter, it will turn out all right in the end.

The problem with this solution is that we have not had that initial encounter! Indeed in the Book of Job it is precisely such an encounter that the afflicted Job seems to be seeking: 'If only I could talk to Him . . . .' This is a persistent problem in Judeo-Christian theism because the encounter with God is a post-mortem situation. But as has often been pointed out, the situation within Hinduism in general, as distinguished from Hindu theism, is very different in this respect. Pre-mortem salvation is possible, indeed it is the primary form of salvation in the schools of Sāṅkhya and Advaita Vedānta. Its existence in the latter, that is, Advaita Vedānta, is widely recognised:

> The characteristics of the liberated man, the one 'released while living' (*jīvan-mukta*), are stated in many texts of the Vedantic school. They represent the supreme ideal of the 'divine man on earth' as envisioned in the penitential groves – an image of human majesty and serenity that has inspired India for centuries. One may compare and contrast it with the various ideals for man that have served to shape in other lands the raw materials of life: the Hebrew patriarch, the Greek athlete-philosopher, the Roman soldier-stoic, the knight of the chivalrous Middle Ages, the eighteenth-century gentleman, the objective man of science, the monk, the warrior, the king, or the Confucian scholar-sage.[63]

This concept of *jīvanmukti* or living liberation makes verification and falsification of religious propositions a living reality. All that one requires is enough provisional faith to take the basic statements of the system seriously enough to put them into practice. The truth or otherwise of the statements is then verified, or falsified, in this very life. The procedure is analogous to a scientific experiment. A schoolboy reads in his textbook of science that water is H_2O. He has enough confidence in his textbook and teacher to conduct the experiment. At the end of the experiment, if successful (and here the text and the teacher assist him), he knows for himself that water is H_2O. He does not need faith in the text or the teacher any more; he knows it for himself. Even during the course of the experiment only *provisional* faith in the teacher and the text were required. One could even be sceptical as to the *results* of the experiment but not as to the method, otherwise even the experiment would not be carried out. This analogy between scientific and religious procedures in some forms of Hinduism can be sustained quite well; where it breaks down is in the public nature of the scientific experiment and the private nature of the claim to realisation. This has led to some discussions of how one, on the outside, can determine if someone is liberated on the inside, and indications have been given, but the issue remains. Nevertheless the structure of verification and falsification procedure in science, and in Hindu systems which accept living liberation, is remarkably parallel.

The problem arises in the context of Hindu theism which by and large does not admit the doctrine of living liberation. It has been claimed of some schools that they do, and one,[64] that of Caitanya, is sometimes cited. But the situation in this respect is not entirely clear.[65] I would now like to develop a clear-cut and unambiguous case for the existence of living liberation in theistic Hinduism.

One must begin by pointing out that the schools of Sāṅkhya and Yoga are often hyphenated,[66] so one can never be sure, when the existence of living liberation is admitted with respect to the hyphenated Sāṅkhya-Yoga school,[67] whether it obtains unequivocally in both. I will now try to establish that the school of Yoga *by itself* admits of living liberation or *jīvanmukti*, not figuratively but literally. It can be clearly stated with respect to Yoga by itself that 'the discriminating (*vidvān*) self becomes liberated, even while living an embodied life. This is called embodied release (*jīvanmukti*)'[68] – or living liberation. This follows from the commentary of Vyāsa on Yoga-sūtra IV. 30. Vyāsa remarks: *jīvanneva vidvān vimukto bhavati*.[69] That is to say 'the wise man, even while yet alive, is released'.[70] This state is described by scholars of Yoga in various ways. For a traditional description we turn to Nāgeśa who says, while explaining Vyāsa's commentary on Yoga-sūtra IV. 31:

> In this jīvanmukta stage, being freed from all impure afflictions and karmas, the consciousness shines in its infinity. The infiniteness of consciousness is different from the infiniteness of materiality veiled by tamas. In those stages there could be consciousness only with reference to certain things, with reference to which the veil of tamas was raised by rajas. When all veils and impurities are removed, then little is left which is not known. If there were other categories besides the 25 categories, these also would then have been known (*Chāyāvyākhyā*, IV.31).[71]

A modern statement is provided by Mircea Eliade, who thus describes the state of the *jīvanmukta*:

> Clearly, his situation is paradoxical. For he is in life, and yet liberated; he has a body, and yet he knows himself and thereby *is puruṣa*; he lives in duration, yet at the same time shares in immortality; finally, he coincides with all Being, though he is but a fragment of it, etc. But it has been toward the realization of this paradoxical situation that Indian spirituality has tended from its beginnings. What else are the 'men-gods' of whom we spoke earlier, if not the 'geometric point' where the divine and the human coincide, as do being and nonbeing, eternity and death,

> the whole and the part? And, more perhaps than any other civilization, India has always lived under the sign of 'men-gods'.[72]

It is clear, then, that living liberation is admitted in Yoga. Now Yoga is also theistic as distinguished from Sāṅkhya.[73] Do we then not have here a case of living liberation in association with theism?

The problem is the degree of association of theism with Yoga, not the fact. Most scholars tend to regard the inclusion of faith in God as a means to the end of self-realisation, and draw attention to the marginal or at least practical and preliminary nature of theism in the Yoga system.[74] In this context one must refer to Yoga-sūtra I.23 where devotion to God does not appear as 'a part of the preliminary discipline' but wherein such devotion to God is represented as a means, alternative to Yogic practice, of attaining samādhi and, through it, kaivalya'.[75] The fact that the same word *Īśvarapraṇidhāna* is used here as in II.32 where the five preliminary *niyamas* are mentioned has led some scholars into even seeing a 'contradiction' here. But the overall picture of theism in Yoga is best presented thus:

> According to the training so far described for attaining spiritual aloofness, devotion to God occupies a subordinate place. Its practice has to be followed by the discipline of the remaining six 'limbs' (*aṅgas*), beginning with bodily postures (*āsana*) and ending with mental concentration (*samādhi*). Patañjali recognizes not only this discipline for securing freedom, but also an alternative one of devotion to God (Iśvara) and communion with him which, without all the elaborate preparation of *yoga*, qualifies for release. That is, apart from serving as an ideal, God, out of his abundant mercy which is one of his perfections, sympathizes with suffering men and helps them in attaining spiritual freedom, if they only trust in him and meditate upon him. It is described as the easier of the two paths, obviously for those who can rest in faith; and it corresponds to the 'path of devotion' (*bhakti-yoga*).[76]

If then man can attain realisation through devotion to God in Yoga; and if this realisation is of the nature of living liberation; and if being liberated involves the removal of all 'veils and impurities' and little is 'left which is not known', then God is bound to be known. Thus it can be claimed that in the Yoga system of Hindu thought God *can* be known in a pre-mortem state.

Nevertheless it is true that most of Hindu theism associates salvation with the idea of communion with God in a post-mortem state. We must then turn to the third solution which has been suggested in the context of the application of the ideas of verification and falsification to theological statements. This approach is associated with the name of John H. Hick who refers to it as the idea of eschatological verification.[77] He presents it with the help of the following preliminary points:

(1) That 'the common feature in all cases of verification in the ascertaining of truth is the removal of grounds for rational doubt', so that 'the verification of a factual assertion is not the same as a logical demonstration of it'.
(2) Verification may require the fulfilment of certain prerequisites. To cite a trifling example: to ascertain whether there is a chair in the next room may involve having to go there.
(3) By the expression 'verifiable' one tends to mean 'publicly verifiable', which in turn means verifiability by everyone in principle. The number of people who *actually* do such verification depends on several factors.
(4) A proposition may be verifiable but not falsifiable. 'Consider, for example, the proposition that "there are three successive sevens in the decimal determination of Π". So far as the value of Π has been worked out, it does not contain a series of three sevens; but since the operation can proceed *ad infinitum* it will always be true that a triple seven may occur at a point not yet reached in anyone's calculations. Accordingly, the proposition may one day be verified if it is true but can never be falsified if it is false'.
(5) Post-mortem existence represents 'another instance of a proposition which is verifiable if true but not falsifiable if false'.[78]

This idea can now be applied not only to the end of one life, but to the end of history, justifying further its description as eschatological verification in a specifically Christian context. Hick uses an interesting parable of two people journeying to a destination – one in certainty of the destination and the other in doubt about it; 'they do not entertain different expectations about the coming details of the road, but only about its ultimate destination. Yet, when they turn the last corner, it will be apparent that one of them has been right all the time and the other wrong'.[79] Hick goes on to say that this parable

> is designed to make only one point: that Judaic-Christian theism postulates an ultimate unambiguous existence *in patria*, as well as our present ambiguous existence *in via*. There is a state of having arrived as well as a state of journeying, an eternal heavenly life as well as an earthly pilgrimage. The alleged future experience cannot, of course, be appealed to as evidence for theism as a present interpretation of our experience, but it does apparently suffice to render the choice between theism and atheism a real and not merely an empty or verbal choice.[80]

This passage has been cited because several key points are involved even when this concept of eschatological verification is viewed from the point of view of Hindu theism, as distinguished from Hindu thought in general. First, there is no end or eschaton as such in Hinduism. History will not come to an end, ever. So the destinations are *individual* destinations and there is no one final grand moment of destiny for all, a turning point after which all will be revealed to all. One may distinguish here between history and biography. History relates to the whole group, the cosmos, biography to the individual. In Christian eschatology, history and biography coincide. In Hinduism there is a biographical end; but no historical end. An individual's involvement in the process of *saṁsāra* can come to an end, but the process itself is unending. Secondly, it is not entirely clear how the choice between theism and atheism is a real choice. One sees the following difficulties:

(1) One could just journey with an open mind. Let us suppose that three people were travelling instead of two: a theist, an atheist and an agnostic. So the choice is not just between theism and atheism.
(2) It is not the choice which is real, it is the end which is real. For presumably the end is independent of the choices made, it will come anyway. So the real question is: does the theist fare better at the end in any way apart from being able to say 'I told you so!' If the atheist, let us say, is a 'pious atheist', then will the end, in the end, be any different for him? A

vital point is involved here from a Hindu perspective: what counts in the end – conduct or belief?

(3) Even if the choice is accepted as real we have the problem of not knowing the nature of the end.

What Hick states is verifiable but not falsifiable; but there are two points to be verified: (a) that there is a grand consummation and (b) that the scenario is going to be what the Christian thinks it is going to be. The atheist may be surprised by the fact *that* there is something at the end, the theist could be as easily surprised by *what* he finds at the end.

V

One may now offer some general comments from the Hindu point of view on the general question of verification and falsification. In this respect the following points emerge from a consideration of the Hindu point of view.

(1) Western philosophy of religion has not clearly identified the general philosophical issue involved in the discussion of verification and falsification. The general issue is this: is whatever knowledge we gain to be *presumptively* considered valid or invalid? If it is considered valid, then theological propositions may be considered true unless shown to be false. If it is considered presumptively invalid, then they are to be considered false unless shown to be true. Clearly in the present, in the modern cultural climate, theological statements are presumptively regarded as invalid, hence the involvement of the philosophy of religion with verification and falsification. The point may be clarified with an appeal to the legal system. Two positions can be assumed in relation to the accused: (a) he/she may be treated as innocent until proven guilty or (b) he/she may be treated as guilty until proven innocent. It seems that theological statements attract the second option.

Both the views on the validity of knowledge cited above are represented within Hindu thought:

> How is the validity of knowledge to be known? Indian theories of knowledge are divisible broadly into two classes – one maintaining the self-validity (*svataḥ-prāmāṇya*) of knowledge; and the

other contending that it needs to be validated by an extraneous means (*parataḥ-prāmāṇya*). In the former view, whenever knowledge arises, the presumption is that it is right; and verification becomes necessary only when there is some circumstance throwing doubt upon it. In the latter case knowledge by itself guarantees nothing in this respect; and its truth or falsity is to be ascertained through some appropriate test.[81]

(2) It is clear that the tenor of scholarly opinion in the Western philosophy of religion is in favour of *parataḥ-prāmāṇya* (or that knowledge to be true must be validated) when it comes to theological statements. This clearly explains the incorporation within it of the positivist emphasis on verification and falsification. By contrast a substantial body of Hindu opinion, especially that which is allied to Vedānta, favours the opposite view, that of the self-validity of knowledge or *svataḥ-prāmāṇya*. It accepts things as true unless shown to be otherwise. Herein lies the key towards the understanding of the curious phenomenon that while the Western philosophy of religion is preoccupied with issues of verification and falsification, Hindu philosophy seems to be preoccupied with theories of error.[82] This seems to follow naturally from their respective epistemological orientations of false until proven true and true until proven false. Verification and falsification are procedures for establishing truth; theories of error are concerned with explaining falsity.

(3) We may narrow the focus of the discussion further and now relate the issues of verification and falsification to the school of Hindu thought which shares the orientation that knowledge is false until proven true – namely, the Nyāya. According to Nyāya the truth or falsity of knowledge is 'to be determined by practical verification (*saṁvādipravṛtti*). If it is "water" for instance that we think we perceive, the validity of the perception is known by the successful quenching (say) of our thirst by it. If it fails to satisfy this or some other similar test, we conclude that it is invalid.'[83]

In applying this to the present context we run into a problem. Is the existence of God to be proved by successful answer to prayers? Here we need to remind ourselves that Nyāya establishes the existence of God by inference and by scripture, not by perception. Hence the point cannot perhaps be pushed any further along this line. However, a Nyāya view discussed earlier does help in developing another point. One may begin by stating it succinctly and comprehensively:

> Thus the truth or falsity of knowledge is a matter of later inference. It is true if it works; otherwise, it is false. It should, however, be carefully noted that this pragmatic criterion is here only a *test* of truth and does not, as in modern pragmatism, constitute its nature. Unlike the latter, the Nyāya-Vaiśeṣika lays full stress on the cognitive function of *pramāṇa*. Error implies ignorance of the true character of the object given, and the removal of that ignorance is the primary purpose of knowledge. The practical activity to which it leads, and which is here made the criterion of its validity, is only a *further* consequence of it. It implies a motive operating subsequently to cognition, viz. to attain what is liked or to avoid what is disliked. In the absence of such a motive, knowledge will not lead to any practical activity; but its logical quality is not thereby affected.[84]

The implications of this view in the context of our discussion may now be drawn out. It should be noted that the accent is on *application* rather than verification and falsification. In other words, if we apply pragmatic rather than positivist criteria to theological statements, Hare's *bliks* start making much more sense, as also the Hindu approach in general. At the same time one can see how the discussion of the existence of God can be held at the logical level without involving any practical application, though such a position may not be fully satisfying for many.

(4) One final point remains to be made. The previous discussion dealt mainly with cognition and this is helpful if religious propositions are held to be cognitive. It may be recalled here that religious propositions are held to be factual statements in Hindu thought as well, but only about the suprasensuous realm. But now if we extend the scope of our consideration from Nyāya to Vedānta, a vital question is raised, for then 'the question that would arise is: how are we to know that cognition corresponds to reality? We cannot get outside of ourselves; and so, there can be no direct evidence of correspondence between mind and object'.[85]

When we establish the truth or falsity of a statement by verification or falsification all we establish is the fact that the statement corresponds to cognition: but 'how are we to know that cognition corresponds to reality' for our cognition is limited by our sense-perception, but is religious reality limited by it?

VI

The chapter has hitherto dealt with the influence of logical positivism on the philosophy of religion; and the reaction of the philosophers of religion to this influence. The response from a Hindu standpoint to this reaction on the part of the philosophy of religion was also considered. In this final section we may now consider the response of Hindu thought to logical positivism.

In our age, dominated as it is by science and technology, the philosophical doctrine of logical positivism must be taken into account. As we try to do so, however, we run into an initial difficulty.

> From the philosophical writings of Indians today one gains the impression that Indian thinkers are either critical or unenthusiastic about the modern Western philosophical trends of logical positivism, existentialism and the philosophy of mere analysis. Whether this is due to traditional bias or to genuine philosophical insight is hard to determine.[86]

Nonetheless a few comments may be made.

The fact that the Judeo-Christian tradition has been prone to factual assertions leaves it particularly open to the application of logical positivism. The application of logical positivism could start with the incidents recorded in the Bible, but will be confined here to the study of theism. The Hindu religious tradition has *not* been prone to make factual assertions in the usual sense, indeed, it demythologised the Vedas centuries before Bultmann[87] but a few additional points need to be made. First the logical positivists could easily assume that the question of truth or falsity of factual assertions does not apply to religion because it is based on feeling. This, however, would be an error, as such feeling would have a referent whose truth or otherwise could be called in question. 'All the mystics and saints attest to the fact that religious faith is cognitive'. This is what we would mean by factual assertion. Moreover, 'just because the disclosure of God is non-inferential, it cannot be devoid of intellectual content'. The intellectual fact could even be primary. Here again factuality of a kind is involved. Moreover, even if the experience was primarily one of feeling,

> the feeling of dependence presupposes that there is an "*Other*", an independent Reality, which can be depended upon, just as

> the feeling of gratitude presupposes our knowledge of someone, to whom we ought to be grateful; and the knowledge of a person worthy of adoration must be antecedent to the act of worship, though worship may confirm and deepen that knowledge. We must therefore conclude that in religious experience, man is aware of a presence that compels recognition, though it can only be imperfectly expressed in words.[88]

Secondly a further point calls for clarification. The determination of the truth or falsity of a statement may require rather forbidding pre-conditions, but that by itself does not render it unverifiable. In most schools of Hindu thought, for instance, 'it is only by resorting to spiritual discipline and a stern ethical attitude of mind that an individual realizes the truth of transcendence, and having once attained it he is capable of communicating it even through speech, though imperfectly'.[89]

Thirdly in Hindu theism, tests have been laid down for the proof not of theism, but of devotion to God. Should that not be considered verifiable – not theism but theistic devotion?

Fourthly it will probably be fair to say that only scientists in many cases will be able to verify what *other* scientists have said. Should it not then be a point for consideration in the philosophy of religion that only some men of religion could verify the claims of other men of religion?

Fifthly an affirmation may be checked for its truth or falsity but here again, in certain situations, difficulties could arise. Suppose I said this room is cold. True or false? For someone who has just come in from the outside, where it's colder, the room would be warm. If it was warmer outside, the room would be cold. Factual statements about experience, therefore, have to be considered carefully. In the light of this the logical positivist idea of 'experienceable difference' also requires further examination. Hick speaks of

> the famous rabbit which at one time haunted philosophical discussions at Oxford. It is a very special rabbit – invisible, intangible, inaudible, weightless, and odorless. When the rabbit has been defined by all these negations, does it still make sense to insist that such a creature exists? It is difficult to avoid a negative answer. It seems clear that when every experienceable feature has been removed, there is nothing left about which we can make assertions.[90]

But this example is too abstract. Let us revert to the example of the cold room. Anyone entering it and finding it warm or cold would admit to perceiving an 'experienceable difference'. Would the logical positivist? Even if it is admitted that an 'experienceable difference' exists, there is the problem that it is contradictory – one person finds the room hot and another cold. One may now refer to the temperature as the neutral arbiter. But temperature must make an experienceable difference and it can only do that by being experienced, which may lead to contradictory results. Moreover, how are we to decide at what exact point does something 'warm' become 'cold' or vice-versa? So the judgemental element has not been removed, only thrust further backwards.

Sixthly the results which follow when philosophers of religion apply logical positivist procedures on their (philosophers') own terms may be examined. It was pointed out earlier how Udayana cited the non-proof of atheism as one of the proofs of the existence of God. So the question may now be posed: can theism be decisively refuted? Herein a Christian argument has been suggested based on God as a loving father by Anthony Flew, which was mentioned earlier and is cited in full now:

> Now it often seems to people who are not religious as if there was no conceivable event or series of events the occurrence of which would be admitted by sophisticated religious people to be a sufficient reason for conceding 'There wasn't a God after all' or 'God does not really love us then'. Someone tells us that God loves us as a father loves his children. We are reassured. But then we see a child dying of inoperable cancer of the throat. His earthly father is driven frantic in his efforts to help, but his Heavenly Father reveals no obvious sign of concern. Some qualification is made – God's love is 'not a merely human love' or it is 'an inscrutable love', perhaps – and we realize that such sufferings are quite compatible with the truth of the assertion that 'God loves us as a father (but, of course . . .)'. We are reassured again. But then perhaps we ask: what is this assurance of God's (appropriately qualified) love worth, what is this apparent guarantee really a guarantee against? Just what would have to happen not merely (morally and wrongly) to tempt but also (logically and rightly) to entitle us to say 'God does not love us' or even 'God does not exist?' I therefore put . . . the simple central question, 'What would have to occur or to have occurred

to constitute for you a disproof of the love of, or of the existence of, God?'[91]

It will soon be apparent that this argument will not apply in the Hindu case as the doctrine of karma is likely to take care of it. Moreover according to Nyāya,

> God's action in creation is indeed caused by compassion. But we must not forget that the idea of creation which consists only of happiness is inconsistent with the nature of things. Certain eventual differences in the form of happiness or misery are bound to arise out of the good or bad actions of the beings who are to be created. It cannot be said that this will limit God's independence in so far as His compassionate creative act depends on the actions of other beings. One's own body does not hinder one. Rather, it helps one to act and achieve one's end. In a like manner, the created world does not hinder and limit God, but serves as the means for the realization of God's moral ends and rational purposes.[92]

However let the Hindu option not be pressed into service. Then a strange consequence seems to ensue. Anthony Flew is in effect arguing against the existence of God by suggesting that no conceivable event could falsify that belief. By altering the term of reference, his argument can be made to support the case for theism, by maintaining that if atheism cannot falsify God's existence (instead of theism having to prove it) it has to be accepted as valid.

Finally let us consider the upshot of it all. In a sense we are back to square one. Does God exist? But there is more: we are beginning to ask, under the influence of logical positivists, how is life affected by the belief or disbelief in the existence of God? Now we get into a logically interesting situation. Suppose I start believing in God and this changes my life? Now an 'experienceable difference' has taken place in life *without* the truth or falsity of the statement having been established.

This paradox has a very interesting implication for Hinduism. It is widely felt in the Indic religious tradition that what you know is a function of what you are. So whether you are able to verify whether someone is coming from a distance is a function of your eye-sight. This would not be the case if you were blind. To take a less trivial example: whether you are able to establish that certain particles exist depends on the hard work you put in as a scientist to prove it. Now the point may be stretched even further through the anecdote of the golf-playing Swami. The Swami was playing golf and hit the ball rather far off the grass. When he asked the disciple how far it was the disciple gave him the correct answer, which was not very encouraging. Thereupon the Swami said: you are not supposed to tell the truth but what is uplifting! The anecdote can easily support lying, but the point is that the *factual result would have been affected by the non-factual statement*. The basic Hindu insight here seems to be that where philosophy cannot provide a definite answer, it is perhaps better to be guided by psychology, and provide the wholesome answer.

One is still not sure whether it is 'traditional bias' or 'genuine philosophical insight' which leaves many Hindu thinkers cold when logical positivism is extended into the religio-spiritual area, but some of the points mentioned above may indicate the kind of problems which keep them from rushing in.

Notes and References

1. John H. Hick, *Philosophy of Religion*, 3rd edn (Englewood Cliffs, New Jersey: Prentice-Hall, 1983) p. 94.
2. Ibid.
3. K. Satchidananda Murty, *Revelation and Reason in Advaita Vedānta* (New York: Columbia University Press, 1959) p. 306.
4. Ibid., pp. 237–9.
5. Ibid., pp. 305–6. Murty does not seem to distinguish between the two arguments clearly, namely, (a) that scriptures are valid because they are the word of God and (b) they are valid as the reports of competent and trustworthy people.
6. Ibid.
7. Ibid., p. 307.
8. Ibid., p. 308.
9. Idem.
10. Ibid., p. 309.
11. Ibid., p. 308.
12. John H. Hick, op. cit., pp. 94–5.
13. Ibid., p. 95.
14. Pratima Bowes, *The Hindu Religious Tradition: A Philosophical Approach* (London: Routledge and Kegan Paul, 1977) p. 282.
15. Ibid., p. 285.
16. Ibid.
17. Ibid., p. 286.

18. Ibid., p. 287.
19. Ibid., p. 288.
20. R. K. Tripathi, *Problems of Philosophy and Religion* (Varanasi: Banaras Hindu University, 1971) pp. 88ff; Swami Nikhilananda (tr.), *The Gospel of Sri Ramakrishna* (New York: Ramakrishna-Vivekananda Center, 1942) p. 192, etc.
21. See Bhagavadgītā II.54–72; XII.13–19; XIV.21–6.
22. Karl H. Potter, *Presuppositions of India's Philosophies* (Englewood Cliffs, New Jersey: Prentice-Hall, 1963) p. 26.
23. Ibid.
24. Ibid., p. 27.
25. Ibid.
26. Ibid.
27. Ibid., p. 30.
28. Ibid., p. 31.
29. Ibid., p. 31.
30. Ibid.
31. Ibid.
32. Ibid., p. 32.
33. Ibid.
34. Ibid.
35. John H. Hick, op. cit., pp. 95–6.
36. As quoted ibid., p. 96.
37. Ibid.
38. Ibid.
39. Ibid.
40. Louis Fischer, *The Life of Mahatma Gandhi* (New York: Harper & Brothers, 1950) p. 323.
41. Ibid.
42. R. K. Prabhu and Ravindra Kelekar (eds), *Truth Called Them Differently* (*Tagore-Gandhi Controversy*) (Ahmedabad: Navajivan Publishing House, 1961) p. 115.
43. Louis Fischer, op. cit., p. 323.
44. Ibid.
45. Quoted in John H. Hick, *Philosophy of Religion*, p. 97
46. Nahum N. Glatzer (ed.), *The Dimensions of Job* (New York: Schocken Books, 1969) p. 211.
47. Prakash Chandra Gupta, *Prem Chand* (New Delhi: Sahitya Akademi, 1968) pp. 30–1.
48. Ibid., p. 51.
49. Hans Raj 'Rahbar', *Prem Chand, His Life and Work* (Delhi: Atma Ram and Sons, 1957) p. 146.
50. M. Hiriyanna, *The Essentials of Indian Philosophy* (London: George Allen & Unwin, 1949) p. 164.
51. Eliot Deutsch, *Advaita Vedānta: A Philosophical Reconstruction* (Honolulu: East-West Center Press, 1969) p. 43.
52. This seems to be implied in Eliot Deutsch and J. A. B. van Buitenen, *A Source Book of Advaita Vedānta* (Honolulu: The University Press of Hawaii, 1971) p. 36.

53. John H. Hick, op. cit., p. 97.
54. Śvetāśvatara Upanisad I.2.
55. R. M. Hare quoted in John H. Hick, op. cit., p. 98.
56. Ibid., p. 98.
57. Ibid., p. 98–9.
58. Ibid., p. 99.
59. Ibid., p. 98.
60. Pratima Bowes, *The Hindu Religious Tradition: A Philosophical Approach*, p. 287; and other works.
61. John H. Hick, op. cit., p. 99.
62. Ibid.
63. Heinrich Zimmer, (ed. Joseph Campbell), *Philosophies of India* (New York: Meridian Books, 1964) p. 441. By 'texts of Vedantic school' obviously those of Advaita Vedānta are meant.
64. Pratima Bowes, op. cit., p. 235.
65. Haridas Bhattacharyya (ed.), *The Cultural Heritage of India*, vol. III (Calcutta: Ramakrishna Mission Institute of Culture, 1953 [first published 1937]) pp. 376–7.
66. M. Hiriyanna, *Outlines of Indian Philosophy* (London: George Allen & Unwin, 1964 [first published 1932]) ch. XI; and other works.
67. Ibid., p. 297.
68. Jadunath Sinha, *A History of Indian Philosophy*, vol. II (Calcutta: Central Book Agency, 1952) p. 174.
69. *Pātañjalayogasūtrāṇi* (Poona: Ānandāśma Series 47, 1978) p. 203.
70. James Haughton Woods (tr.), *The Yoga-System of Patañjali* (Delhi: Motilal Banarsidass, 1966 [first published by Harvard Press, 1914]) p. 341.
71. Surendranath Dasgupta, *Yoga as Philosophy and Religion* (Delhi: Motilal Banarsidass, 1973 [first published in London, 1924]) pp. 118–19.
72. Mircea Eliade, (tr. Willard R. Trask) *Yoga Immortality and Freedom* (New York: Pantheon Books. 1958) p. 95.
73. T. M. P. Mahadevan, *Outlines of Hinduism* (Bombay: Chetana, 1971) p. 129.
74. Mircea Eliade, op. cit., p. 96; Satischandra Chatterjee and Dhirendramohan Datta, *An Introduction to Indian Philosophy* (University of Calcutta, 1968) p. 307; and other works.
75. M. Hiriyanna, *Outlines of Indian Philosophy*, p. 295 fn. 1.
76. M. Hiriyanna, *The Essentials of Indian Philosophy*, p. 126. It should be added that not all commentators accept the 'alternative character' of devotion to God (ibid., ch. V, p. 207 n. 13). It was Hiriyanna himself who saw the contradiction mentioned earlier. As the present book is subsequent to the one cited in the previous note we take this passage as representing his mature conclusion in the matter.
77. John H. Hick, op. cit., pp. 100–2.
78. Ibid., pp. 100–1.
79. Ibid., p. 101.
80. Ibid., pp. 101–2.
81. M. Hiriyanna, *The Essentials of Indian Thought*, p. 98. Also see Charles

A. Moore (ed.), *The Indian Mind* (Honolulu: University of Hawaii Press, 1967) pp. 120–1.
82. See Bijayananda Kar, *Theories of Error in Indian Philosophy: An Analytical Study* (New Delhi: Ajanya Publications, 1978); and other works.
83. M. Hiriyanna, *The Essentials of Indian Philosophy*, p. 98.
84. Ibid., pp. 98–9.
85. T. M. P. Mahadevan, op. cit., p. 106.
86. Charles A. Moore (ed.), op. cit., p. 39.
87. K. Satchidananda Murty, *Revelation and Reason in Advaita Vedānta* (New York: Columbia University Press, 1959) p. 219.
88. Ibid., p. 317.
89. Stanley M. Daugert (ed.), I. C. Sharma. *Ethical Philosophies of India*. (New York: Harper & Row, 1965) p. 53.
90. John H. Hick, *Philosophy of Religion*, p. 95.
91. Anthony Flew as quoted in John H. Hick, op. cit., p. 97.
92. Satischandra Chatterjee and Dhirendramohan Datta, *An Introduction to Indian Philosophy* p. 219.

7

Human Destiny: Immortality and Resurrection

IS THE SOUL IMMORTAL?

In Western thought the doctrine of the immortality of the soul goes back to Plato (428/7–348/7 BC). Plato speaks of two worlds, one of the senses, the other of the intellect. The body belongs to the sensible world, sharing its changeability and perishability. The intellect is related to a different realm of the universals. In it are to be found the 'universals' such as goodness and so on, which are eternal as distinguished from acts of goodness which are fleeting. Now Plato argued that if one was given to the contemplation of eternal truths then, upon death, the body will perish but the soul or intellect will pass on to the eternal realm of the universals.

Plato also tried to rationally establish the existence of the soul by arguing that it was a simple substance as opposed to the body which is composite. Only composite substances disintegrate, so the body perishes but the soul cannot. These arguments have generated two counter-arguments in the main: (a) although a 'simple substance cannot disintegrate, consciousness may nevertheless cease to exist through the diminution of its intensity to zero',[1] as Kant argued; (b) the mind may not be a simple entity but a complex unity, as modern psychology seems to suggest.

The evidence from the Nyāya school (by which is meant here the hyphenated *Nyāya-Vaiśeṣika*) on these points, promises to be of considerable interest. The question of universals may first be examined. Universals are regarded as eternal in Nyāya in the sense that while individual cows may be born or may die, cowness is eternal, to put it with pastoral crudeness. The Nyāya view, however, presents a more serious problem from another standpoint. In Nyāya, universals 'are revealed only through the corresponding particulars, and are not found by themselves'.[2] So although goodness is eternal, it can only be revealed through something good. It is important to remember here that when the Nyāya word *sāmānya* is 'rendered by the word "universal"' a 'complete resemblance to the Platonic "idea"'[3] is not implied. 'For instance, particulars are not here viewed as copies of the universal.'[4] Thus in terms of Nyāya categories we have some problems in getting the 'soul' and 'goodness' together by themselves. These difficulties are purely logical, however, as substance (soul) and quality (goodness) are inseparable. But at this point a substantial difficulty arises. The soul cannot perceive its quality of goodness (*dharma*), though inherent in it, without the mind (*manas*). In Platonic terms it amounts to saying that both 'soul' and 'intellect' as two distinct entities are required for the perception of 'goodness'. A further point of interest is that universals are gradable in Nyāya as lowest, intermediate and highest; the highest being Being (*sattā*); but the 'universals do not come into existence (*sattā*). These do not exist in time and space, but have being and *subsist* in substance, attribute and action'.[5] The 'idea' of Being does not seem to have been considered by Plato.

The criticisms of the Platonic position find an uncanny resonance in Nyāya. For instance, the Kantian view that consciousness could be reduced to zero is actually accepted as the condition of the soul in the state of salvation which in this school is 'not a positive state of happiness but a negative experience of the total absence of pain. The reason why the goal is so conceived is that there can be no happiness without an admixture of pain'.[6] It should be noted though that the non-existence of consciousness does not imply non-existence of the soul. Actually, in Nyāya, consciousness is 'an accidental attribute of the soul'.[7]

We turn now to the criticism directed at the Platonic idea of the soul by modern psychologists who prefer to regard the mind as a complex unity rather than a simple entity. The mind (*manas*) is recognised as atomic in structure in Nyāya.

The remarkable result of this comparison between the Platonic idea of the soul (and its criticisms) with the concepts of the Nyāya-Vaiśeṣika system is that we find the concept of the soul being retained in Nyāya with the criticisms of that Platonic concept having already been accommodated into the system! This consequence seems to follow from the peculiarity of the Nyāya-Vaiśeṣika system that the soul or

> the self is the basis of psychic life, but that life is only adventitious to it. The necessary condition for the appearance of psychic features in the self is its association with *manas*. For these reasons, it would perhaps be better to describe the two together as really constituting the self in the common acceptation of that term. But we should remember that the conception of *manas*, taken by itself, is equally non-spiritual. The true self is thus broken up here, we may say, in two 'selfless elements'.[8]

This is about as far as Platonic, Kantian and modern psychological perspectives could be integrated. The result does not seem to be particularly appealing.

The body/soul dichotomy was given a fresh lease of life by René Descartes (1596–1650), but has largely been abandoned by modern philosophers as there seems to be no real way of distinguishing the mind from the soul. However if the mind could somehow be shown to be independent of the body, at least for certain durations, then the first tentative steps towards the recognition of the soul could be taken, *pace* the Buddhists.

One may begin by recognising and emphasising the obvious, that while on the one hand the outside world is known to us through the mind, and not the body, we have no experience of having a mind apart from the body. It is this inseparability of the body and mind which is the real issue. We know that the body can function without a conscious mind as in sleep, especially deep sleep, or that the mind can function without an awareness of the body, as in deep thought. But we do not know whether they can exist in separation. Thus we are left with the following broad options: (a) that the body generates the mind along with itself; (b) or the mind (soul) generates (Hinduism) or occupies (Christianity) the body for the duration of its existence; (c) or the dichotomy is false and body and soul/mind are merely two aspects of a single psycho-physical organism.

These may respectively be designated as the materialist, the spiritual and the Hebraic views of the body/soul relationship.

The Indian materialists have held several views on the body/soul relationship within the basic framework of their inseparability. Some held that the body itself is the soul;[9] others that there is a soul apart from the body that does not survive physical death;[10] yet others that the soul is not different from the mind[11] and so on.[12] Both the Indian materialists and the Hebrews identified body and soul, but the direction of the identification is different. It is a case of the identification of the *soul* with body in the Indian case and *body* with soul in the Hebraic case. This may help explain the divergent moral destinies of the two groups. The Indian materialists veered towards atheistic hedonism; the Hebrews turned in the direction of a theistic morality.

It will be interesting to consider some of the Hindu arguments in favor of the autonomous character of consciousness. The use of the words mind and soul have been deliberately avoided here for two reasons. First because the independence of consciousness from the body is the primary issue and its identification as a feature of mind or soul a secondary one; and secondly because in this way both theologians and psychologists can be kept interested in the discussion. The main arguments which may be considered in this context are the following:[13]

(1) 'If consciousness be a property of the body, it should be either essential to it or accidental. If the former, it should be inseparable from the body and last as long as it does; but it does not, for in a swoon or in dreamless sleep the body is seen without it. If the latter, it implies another agency (*upādhi*) at work in producing consciousness and cannot, therefore, be wholly ascribed to the body.'[14] It may be added that, if identical with the body, it should last as long as the body lasts, but a dead body is devoid of consciousness.[15] No one, it seems, suggested the following argument: if consciousness is a property of the body it should be co-extensive with the body. But we have no living consciousness in hair, nails and so on, in the sense that if they are cut consciousness is not disturbed. It is clear that consciousness does not characterise the entire body (just as it does not characterise it all the time). Can they then be regarded as identical or even co-extensive?

(2) The existence of dream-cognitions adds another dimension to the issue. There are, first, dream cognitions when the body is not conscious, as in sleep. Secondly, a particular dream cognition may be examined. Let us suppose someone dreams that he is a tiger. When he awakens, he 'owns the dream experience while disowning the dream body, say that of a tiger'.[16] It could, of course, be argued that the dream state is different from the waking state, but this seems to

> create further problems. If consciousness is identical with the body then how do we explain the fact that *one* body experiences *three* states of 'consciousness' – waking, dreaming and deep sleep? It could be argued that each has a corresponding bodily manifestation; namely, physical awareness, rapid eye movement and physical rest; then it means that all consciousness must have a corresponding physical phenomenon. If now someone loses his arm in an accident how does he know he does not have an arm? The likely answer is: through memory. But memory implies transference of mental impressions. How is this *constant* memory to be reconciled with a changing physical body? Instead of prolonging the discussion[17] it seems reasonable to conclude that some states or contents of consciousness can be described without reference to bodily states; and so it must remain an open question whether consciousness is independent of the body or not.

In this respect the elaboration of a metaphor suggested by Vācaspati Miśra is helpful.[18] It has to do with the relationship between light and visual perception. One cannot see without light; in fact how well one sees and how much one sees depends on light and indeed seeing without light is inconceivable. Are we to deduce then that 'seeing' or visual perception is a property of light?

RESURRECTION

The idea of post-mortem survival in Judaism, it appears, underwent change with the passage of time. The original idea seems to have been one of attaining immortality through membership of the Jewish nation 'as an organism that continued through the centuries while successive generations lived and died'.[19] When examined in the light of Hindu thought this idea calls forth two responses. First the idea of surviving through one's successors is also found in ancient Hindu thought, though it did not take the form of immortality through survival as a member of a nation, but rather through one's lineage. For there are passages which declare 'that in the son the father is born again, an idea which is not in itself strictly reconcilable with the view that the soul transmigrates on death',[20] which became the standard Hindu view in the course of time. Secondly, from the Hindu viewpoint the Judaic concept of survival through a community can be brought into relation with the Platonic view of survival through living in a world of 'goodness', and so on, through the category of universals. In the Nyāya-Vaiśeṣika view of universals, the Jewish *community* (*jāti*) would qualify as a universal, the members of which live and die but which by itself is eternal. Thus the Hindu view here has the curious implication of bringing two very divergent forms of post-mortem survival into some kind of a relationship.

With the diaspora and the break-up of the Jewish nation the locus of salvation is said to have shifted to the individual. It is in this context that concepts of survival through belief in after-life in some form emerged. It is also here that the contrast between survival through an immortal soul and survival through a reconstituted body emerges. This latter view has been examined by John H. Hick[21] in its triple version: Hebraic, Christian (Irenaean) and Christian (Pauline). We shall address ourselves only to the idea common to all of these, namely that 'death is something real and fearful. It is not thought to be like walking from one room to another, or like taking off an old coat and putting on a new one. It means sheer unqualified extinction – passing out from the lighted circle of life into "death's dateless night".'[22] And that 'only through the creative love of God can there be a new existence beyond the grave'.[23]

Hick notes that a 'major problem confronting any such doctrine is that of providing criteria of personal identity to link the earthly life and the resurrection life'.[24] He develops this point with the help of the parable of John Smith. In this parable three situations are visualised: each with increasing degree of complexity. Here is the first situation.

> Suppose, first, that someone – John Smith – living in the United States were suddenly and inexplicably to disappear before the eyes of his friends, and that at the same moment an exact replica of him were inexplicably to appear in India. The person who appears in India is exactly similar in both physical and mental characteristics to the person who disappeared in America. There is continuity of memory, complete similarity of bodily features including fingerprints, hair and eye coloration, and stomach contents, and also of beliefs, habits, emotions, and mental dispositions. Further, the 'John Smith' replica thinks of himself as

> being the John Smith who disappeared in the United States. After all possible tests have been made and have proved positive, the factors leading his friends to accept 'John Smith' as John Smith would surely prevail and would cause them to overlook even his mysterious transference from one continent to another, rather than treat 'John Smith,' with all of John Smith's memories and other characteristics, as someone other than John Smith.[25]

This is a case of mere relocation. It may be compared with the next situation involving reincarnation.

> Suppose, second, that our John Smith, instead of inexplicably disappearing, dies, but that at the moment of his death a 'John Smith' replica, again complete with memories and all other characteristics, appears in India. Even with the corpse on our hands, we would, I think, still have to accept this 'John Smith' as the John Smith who had died. We would just have to say that he had been miraculously re-created in another place.[26]

Such reincarnation may now be compared with resurrection, Irenaean style:

> Now suppose, third, that on John Smith's death the 'John Smith' replica appears, not in India, but as a resurrection replica in a different world altogether, a resurrection world inhabited only by resurrected persons. This world occupies its own space distinct from that with which we are now familiar. That is to say, an object in the resurrection world is not situated at any distance or in any direction from the objects in our present world, although each object in either world is spatially related to every other object in the same world.[27]

Hick stops here. But let us follow John Smith into another situation. This time he is resurrected and becomes immortal. Now

> Just try to think of what is left of Mr. Smith after he has become immortal. His body would obviously be gone. With the body his instincts would have disappeared – since they are bound up with his glands, with the needs of his tissues, in short with the body. His mind also, as he knows it, would have to be sacrificed. Because this mind of ours is bound up with bodily processes, its

> operations are based on the data provided by the bodily organs of sense, and it reveals its impermanence by incessantly and restlessly jumping from one thing to another. With the mind would go his sense of logical consistency. As a matter of fact, Mr. John Smith, turned immortal, would not recognize himself at all. He would have lost everything that made him recognisable to himself and to others.[28]

One can see how the question of personal identity becomes increasingly more complex. Herein the general Hindu position that the gaining of the new identity is really the recovery of our original identity provides a fresh perspective on the question. There are problems of identity in all cases of radical transformation, even within a lifetime. Sometimes people even adopt new names to mark that transformation if undertaken consciously. Does it help philosophically to regard the eschatological identity as the true one and the empirical one as in some sense false or at least preparatory? It is a question of whether one chooses to view the situation from the starting point or the end point. The Judeo-Christian tradition uses the former perspective, the Hindu tradition the latter.

One may also note the difference in Christian and Hindu views about the soul and its implications for the question of identity. If the soul is eternal – that is, without birth or death – then its identity is everlasting. Such is the case with Hinduism. But in Christianity the soul is not eternal but immortal – it has a beginning but no end. When the corruptible takes on incorruptibility, the problem of identity is likely to arise with greater force in view of the radical discontinuity involved (as pointed out earlier) than in the case in which the incorruptible sheds its corruption. On the issue of the eternal soul itself even in Plato there are

> two conceptions. There is the doctrine of the *Symposium*, which is not of a future life but of timeless existence, attainable here and now by an escape from the flux of time. There is the other doctrine of the *Phaedo* involving pre-existence and post-existence which are concepts possessing meaning only with regard to the temporal life of the soul.[29]

The first conception is more in keeping with the non-dualistic strain in Hindu thought and the latter with the theistic.

In this context the concept of personality is also of some interest. Heinrich Zimmer has presented an interesting analysis of Indian and Western views[30] with the aid of the etymology of the word *persona*. As is well known *persona* 'means the mask that is worn over the face by the actor on the Greek or Roman stage; the mask "through" (*per*) which he "sounds" (*sonat*) his part'.[31] Thus the term personality must have originally 'implied that people are only impersonating what they seem to be'.[32] Zimmer suggests that Christian philosophy 'has annulled the distinction',[33] the mask and the face have become identical. 'For the Western mind, the personality is eternal',[34] and according to Zimmer this is the 'basic idea in the Christian doctrine of the resurrection of the body, the resurrection being the gaining of our cherished personality in a purified form, worthy to fare before the majesty of the Almighty'.[35] Zimmer goes on to say that for Western man 'to lose his *persona* would mean to lose every hope for a future beyond death. The mask has become for him fused, and confused, with his essence.'[36] In Hindu philosophy, by contrast, the instinct is to keep the distinction between the role and the actor clear and indeed if such clarity could be achieved salvation would ensue.

HEAVEN AND HELL

Whether through resurrection as in the Christian case, or with the passage of the soul as in the Hindu, the human being upon death faces the prospect of ending up either in heaven or hell. The Christian doctrines in this respect are too well known to require elaboration so that one may turn straightaway to an examination of the Hindu ideas of heaven and hell.

The Hindu view of heaven has also undergone transformation, from the original Vedic idea of a kind of a perpetual beer-bash set up by the first mortal in the celestial region, to the present theistic concepts of a transcendental realm of God; except that in Hinduism it is the transcendental realm of a God – Viṣṇu or Śiva primarily. Their Heavens, for which we may use a capital *H*, are beyond the operation of karma and are places of eternal felicity. As has often been pointed out, these may be distinguished from heaven with a small *h* to which one goes through one's *karma* and where one lives only so long as one's good *karma* lasts. We could optionally refer to the former as devotional heavens and to the latter as karmic heavens. This distinction has an interesting implication for the faith versus works controversy in Christianity which did not assume quite the same dimensions in Hindu devotionalism. But in terms of Christianity it is easy to see how the fideists would have insisted that works only led to a temporary sojourn in heaven and faith alone to a lasting one. Actually the possibility of the development of the dual concept of heaven may not be as far-fetched as might appear at first sight. The Kingdom of God on earth and in heaven could easily have provided the seed for such a development.

An interesting feature of the Hindu devotional Heavens is the different degrees of communion the devotees will enjoy in relation to God. It is not quite that we have here a divinised version of the caste system (which does exist in a very different sense.)[37] The type of devotion and the form of *sādhanā,* or spiritual practices, is related to the nature of the union with God. The exact details may vary with the system but the following pattern may be taken as representative.

Type of Practice	Mode of Devotion	Nature of Salvation (*mokṣa*)
(1) external acts of worship (*caryā*)	servant in relation to God (*dāsa*)	residence in the realm of God (*sālokya*)
(2) acts of intimate service to God (*kriyā*)	good son in relation to God (*sat-putra*)	nearness to God (*sāmīpya*)
(3) contemplation and internal worship (*yoga*)	friend in relation to God (*sakhā*)	gaining the form of God (*sārūpya*)
(4) direct knowledge of God (*jñāna*)	God as truth (*sat*)	'union' with God (*sāyujya*)[38]

A few clarifications may be offered now. The word *sāyujya* (from the same root found in the Sanskrit word *yoga* and the English 'yoke') is sometimes used in Hindu non-dualism to represent the 'union' of Ātman and Brahman. It has no such connotation here for 'even in the state of release, the soul is entitatively different from God'.[39] Sometimes another word, *sārṣṭi* is enumerated as a form of salvation. It denotes having the same power as God and is usually subsumed in the four-fold schema of the kind outlined above under *sāyujya*.

The significance of the table may be elaborated with the help of an example. Let us take the case of a student who has been admitted to a university of his choice. The university has a vice-chancellor who is like God on the campus. In such a situation just being on the campus would correspond to *sālokya*; being close to the vice-chancellor to *sāmīpya*; being able to wear the same insignia as he does to *sārūpya*; being able to exercise his powers to *sārṣṭi* and being his close confidant and in constant communion with him to *sāyujya*.

The presence of these distinctions in salvation is interesting for it contrasts with the absence of any such distinction in Hindu monism. Distinctions thus, as a *philosophical* principle, are very important for the theistic systems of Hinduism and seem to find their way into the post-mortem eschatology of these systems. By contrast distinctions among human beings as devotees in the pre-mortem state are minimised as all are seen to be equal in the eyes of God. Somewhat ironically Hindu monism tends to be more inclined to uphold social distinctions, while asserting their complete annulment in the state of salvation.

From heaven we must now turn to the examination of a far less hospitable place, namely, hell, where Satan is said to reign. It is perhaps a point of some interest that there is no Satan or the Devil as such in Hinduism. There are devils, or, more appropriately perhaps, devilish beings and there are the gods and they are pitted against each other quite often in Hindu mythology[40] but there is no Devil opposing God. Interestingly, just as Satan is a fallen angel, both the gods and the demons are of common stock in Hinduism as well.[41] Thus evil lacks a definite focus in Hindu thought and the polarity between good and evil, though recognised, does not crystallise the way it does in the Judeo-Christian tradition. It is perhaps in keeping with the same principle of not merely the relative, but also mutable, nature of good and evil that there is no doctrine of eternal damnation in Hinduism – with one exception which has even been attributed to Christian influence.[42] There are verses of the Gītā (XVI. 19–20) which have been taken to imply it[43] but they have also been interpreted differently. It stands to reason that there is no Hell with a capital *H*, because there is no Devil, but there are karmic hells (with a small *h*) one must go to, to work out bad *karma*. These hells thus are more like purgatories. The Hindu standpoint thus takes a more benevolent view of hell. Hick seems to recommend the demythologisation of hell by taking it to mean 'a continuation of the purgatorial suffering often experienced in life' and as 'leading eventually to the high good of heaven' or by taking it as 'a powerful and pregnant symbol of the grave responsibility inherent in our human freedom in relation to our maker'.[44] One could suggest that being reborn as animals as a result of bad *karma* is comparable to being dispatched to hell as well. It is an interesting coincidence that, just as Hick tries to demythologise hell, Radhakrishnan tries to demythologise animal rebirths. He writes: 'When it is said that the human soul suffers the indignity of animal life, the suggestion is figurative, not literal. It means that it is reborn in an irrational existence comparable to animal life, and not that it is attached to the body of an animal.'[45]

Heinrich Zimmer has some useful comments to offer on why the Christian and the Hindu falls into hell. According to him it is for opposite reasons. For the medieval Christian, personality 'was not lost in death, or purged away by the after-death experiences. Rather, life beyond the grave was but a second manifestation of it.'[46] In the case of evil, it was the realisation of its consequence 'on a broader scale and in a freer style'.[47] In the Hindu case the personalities are not retained. The person becomes the punitive form of life he is in. In Dante's hell the original perpetrators of the crime retain their personality in their punishment;[48] in the Hindu hells 'they are unable to remember any former state'[49] but 'identify themselves exclusively with that which they now are. And this of course is why they are in hell.'[50]

RESUSCITATION

We have talked about heaven and hell, both representing post-mortem habitats of the soul. If we now ask the question: what happens between death and being dispatched to heaven or hell? Then we find ourselves in a limbo of lack of information. The gap has been filled in recent times by numerous studies of what are called near-death experiences. These purport to be the accounts of those who were resuscitated after being declared clinically dead. The accounts are not identical but are sufficiently similar to interest the philosopher of religion. An early researcher in the field, Raymond A. Moody, Jun., has put together the following construct on the basis of 150 cases:

> A man is dying and, as he reaches the point of greatest physical distress, he hears himself pronounced dead by his doctor. He begins to hear an uncomfortable noise, a loud ringing or buzzing, and at the same time feels himself moving very rapidly through a long dark tunnel. After this, he suddenly finds himself outside of his own physical body, but still in the immediate physical environment, and he sees his own body from a distance, as though he is a spectator. He watches the resuscitation attempt from this unusual vantage point and is in a state of emotional upheaval.
>
> After a while, he collects himself and becomes more accustomed to his odd condition. He notices that he still has a 'body,' but one of a very different nature and with very different powers from the physical body he has left behind. Soon other things begin to happen. Others come to meet and to help him. He glimpses the spirits of relatives and friends who have already died, and a loving, warm spirit of a kind he has never encountered before – a being of light – apppears before him. This being asks him a question, nonverbally, to make him evaluate his life and helps him along by showing him a panoramic, instantaneous playback of the major events of his life. At some point he finds himself approaching some sort of barrier or border, apparently representing the limit between earthly life and the next life. Yet, he finds that he must go back to earth, that the time for his death has not yet come. At this point he resists, for by now he is taken up with his experiences in the afterlife and does not want to return. He is overwhelmed by intense feelings of joy, love, and peace. Despite his attitude, though, he somehow reunites with his physical body and lives.
>
> Later he tries to tell others, but he has trouble doing so. In the first place, he can find no human words adequate to describe these unearthly episodes. He also finds that others scoff, so he stops telling other people. Still, the experience affects his life profoundly, especially his views about death and its relationship to life.[51]

What is the philosophical significance of these accounts? The question is a difficult one. Hick offers a balanced reaction:

> Whether or not the resuscitation cases give us reports of the experiences of people who have actually died, and thus provide

information about a life to come, it is at present impossible to determine. Do these accounts describe the first phase of another life, or perhaps a transitional stage before the connection between mind and body is finally broken; or do they describe only the last flickers of dream activity before the brain finally loses oxygen? It is to be hoped that further research may find a way to settle this question.[52]

While the issue awaits scientific arbitration it may not be without interest to consider the matter from a Hindu point of view. The question whether any element of the human personality survives death engaged Hindu thinkers considerably.[53] The consensus seemed to emerge in favour of survival, as is clear from the widespread acceptance of the doctrine of rebirth. But just as the Christian belief in resurrection became widespread without any clear recognition of the exact process involved, the widespread acceptance of rebirth in the Hindu world went hand in hand with a similar lack of exactitude about its mechanism.[54] In this respect the evidence supplied by the recent researches is of interest, even though it does not go so far as either rebirth or resurrection by its very nature. The information offered however is tantalising, especially in relation to the phenomenon of the being of light. We shall not pursue the matter any further except to cite some verses from the Gītā in the near-death context which seem to refer to a being of light. The reader however must be alerted to a vital difference of context: in the Gītā (VIII.8–11) the person about to die is fully aware of his impending demise and is taking certain steps to make the transition smooth:

> Let a man's thoughts be integrated by spiritual exercise and constant striving: let them not stray to anything else at all; so by meditating on the divine exalted Person, [that man to that Person] goes.
> The Ancient Seer, Governor [of all things, yet] smaller than the small, Ordainer of all, in form unthinkable, sun-coloured beyond the darkness, – let a man meditate on Him [as such]. With mind unmoving at the time of passing on, by love-and-devotion integrated and by the power of spiritual exercise too, forcing the breath between the eyebrows duly, so will that man draw nigh to that divine exalted Person.[55]

In these verses the word *divya* is used twice for the being (Person) and in the light of the evidence provided by near-death experiences one must wonder whether the word *divya* here does not just mean divine but rather is to be taken in its etymological sense of the 'shining one' as anticipated by some commentators, a possibility enhanced by the reference to the being's golden colour ('having the colour of the sun'). It must at the same time be admitted that the verses could be interpreted figuratively.

Notes and References

1. John H. Hick, *Philosophy of Religion*, 3rd edn (Englewood Cliffs, New Jersey: Prentice-Hall, 1983) pp. 122–3.
2. M. Hiriyanna, *The Essentials of Indian Philosophy* (London: George Allen & Unwin, 1949) p. 94.
3. M. Hiriyanna, *Outlines of Indian Philosophy* (London: George Allen & Unwin, 1964 [first published 1932]) p. 233.
4. Ibid., p. 233 fn. 1.
5. Satischandra Chatterjee and Dhirendramohan Datta, *An Introduction to Indian Philosophy* (University of Calcutta, 1968) p. 236.
6. T. M. P. Mahadevan, *Outlines of Hinduism* (Bombay: Chetana, 1971) p. 108.
7. Satischandra Chatterjee and Dhirendramohan Datta, op. cit., p. 205.
8. M. Hiriyanna, *The Essentials of Indian Philosophy*, pp. 90–1.
9. Jadunath Sinha, *A History of Indian Philosophy, vol.* I (Calcutta: Sinha Publishing House, 1956) p. 230.
10. Ibid., pp. 244–5.
11. Ibid., p. 256.
12. M. Hiriyanna, *Outlines of Indian Philosophy*, p. 193 fn. 1.
13. For a brief statement see ibid., pp. 192–3; for a more detailed treatment see Jadunath Sinha, op. cit., pp. 254–64.
14. M. Hiriyanna, *Outlines of Indian Philosophy*, p. 192.
15. Jadunath Sinha, op. cit., p. 256.
16. M. Hiriyanna, *Outlines of Indian Philosophy*, p. 192. As Hiriyanna records, the example is given by Vācaspati Miśra.
17. See ibid., p. 255.
18. Ibid., p. 193; Jadunath Sinha, op. cit., vol. I, pp. 258–9.
19. John H. Hick, op. cit., p. 124.
20. Arthur Berriedale Keith, *The Religion and Philosophy of the Veda and the Upanishads* (Cambridge, Mass.: Harvard University Press, 1925) p. 580.
21. John H. Hick, op. cit., pp. 124–6.
22. Ibid., p. 125.
23. Ibid.
24. Ibid.
25. Ibid., pp. 125–6.

26. Ibid., p. 126.
27. John H. Hick, op. cit., p. 126.
28. Edward Conze, *Buddhism: Its Essence and Development* (New York: Harper & Row, 1965) p. 24. Conze uses the example in a different context. It is adapted here to the present context.
29. S. Radhakrishnan, *The Brahma Sūtra: The Philosophy of Spiritual Life* (London: George Allen & Unwin, 1960) p. 185.
30. Heinrich Zimmer, (ed.) Joseph Campbell, *Philosophies of India* (New York: Meridian Books, 1964) pp. 234–40.
31. Ibid., p. 236.
32. Ibid.
33. Ibid.
34. Ibid.
35. Ibid.
36. Ibid., p. 237.
37. See Bṛhadāraṇyaka Upaniṣad I.4.11.
38. Based on T. M. P. Mahadevan, *Outlines of Hinduism*, pp. 171–2. Also see Haridas Bhattacharyya (ed.), *The Cultural Heritage of India*, vol. III (Calcutta: Ramakrishna Mission Insitute of Culture, 1953 [first published 1937]) p. 376; Mariasusai Dhavamony, *Love of God According to Śaiva Siddhānta* (Oxford: Clarendon Press, 1971) pp. 120–1; Surendranath Dasgupta, *A History of Indian Philosophy* (Cambridge University Press, 1922) pp. 317–18.
39. T. M. P. Mahadevan, *Outlines of Hinduism*, p. 172.
40. Benjamin Walker, *The Hindu World*, vol. I (New York: Frederick A. Praeger, 1968) p. 90.
41. Ibid.
42. A. L. Basham, *The Wonder That Was India* (New York: Grove Press, 1954) p. 333.
43. R. C. Zaehner, *The Bhagavadgītā* (London: Oxford University Press, 1969) p. 373.
44. John H. Hick, *Philosophy of Religion*, p. 127.
45. S. Radhakrishnan, op. cit., p. 204.
46. Joseph Campbell (ed), op. cit., p. 235.
47. Ibid.
48. Ibid.
49. Ibid., p. 238.
50. Ibid.
51. Raymond A. Moody, Jun., *Life After Life* (New York: Bantam Books, 1977) pp. 21–3.
52. John H. Hick, op. cit., p. 132.
53. Bṛdhdāraṇyaka Upaniṣad II.4.12 and IV.5.13 have been read as implying non-survival of consciousness after death. That it was an issue is clear from Kaṭha Upaniṣad I.1.20.
54. Arthur Berriedale Keith, *The Religion and Philosophy of the Veda and the Upanishads*, p. 570ff.
55. R. C. Zaehner, op. cit., pp. 263–4.

8

Karma and Reincarnation

I

Albīrūnī, the Muslim savant of the eleventh century, commences one of the chapters of his well-known book on India with the following comment:

> As *the word of confession*, 'There is no god but God, Muḥammad is his prophet,' is the shibboleth of Islam, the Trinity that of Christianity, and the institute of the Sabbath that of Judaism, so metempsychosis is the shibboleth of the Hindu religion. Therefore he who does not believe in it does not belong to them, and is not reckoned as one of them.[1]

The remark is not entirely true, as some sects usually considered Hindu do not subscribe to the doctrine of karma and reincarnation[2] and some religions of Indian origin other than Hinduism such as Buddhism[3] and Jainism[4] do so, yet it serves to highlight the centrality of the doctrine of karma and reincarnation in the Indian milieu.[5] Scholars of comparative religion have contrasted the Hindu idea of reincarnation of the soul with the Western idea of the resurrection of the body,[6] and the concept has recently received much scholarly attention.[7]

II

Western philosophers of religion like John H. Hick have examined the ideas of karma and reincarnation critically and have identified various versions of the doctrine.[8] The central theme of the doctrine is that

> whatever action is done by an individual leaves behind it some sort of a potency which has the power to ordain for him joy or

> sorrow in the future according as it is good or bad. When the fruits of the actions are such that they cannot be enjoyed in the present life or in a human life, the individual has to take another birth as a man or any other being in order to suffer them.[9]

Thus the 'three essential constituents' of a karma theory may be presented in two different ways:

> A: (1) causality (ethical or non-ethical, involving one life or several lives); (2) ethicization (the belief that good and bad acts lead to certain results in one life or several lives); (3) rebirth. B: (1) explanation of present circumstances with reference to previous actions, including (possibly) actions prior to birth; (2) orientation of present actions toward future ends, including (possibly) those occurring after death; (3) moral basis on which action past and present is predicated.[10]

John H. Hick has identified three versions of the doctrine of karma and reincarnation just outlined. These he identifies as: (a) the popular concept; (b) the Vedantic conception; and (c) a demythologised interpretation.

Before we proceed to analyse these three conceptions of the doctrine, however, it will be useful to pause to define our terms of reference as the subject is a vast one. I suggest the following. It will soon be shown that the absence of a doctrine of karma and reincarnation in Western thought creates certain problems. It seems a reasonable procedure then to proceed as follows: each of the three conceptions of the doctrine should be examined for the extent and degree to which they really take care of the problems that are created by the absence of the doctrine in Western thought.

What then are the problems that a philosopy of religion faces in the absence of a doctrine of karma and reincarnation? Let us begin by taking

> note of the main difficulty that Indians see in the western assumption. They point to the immense inequalities of human birth. One person is born with a healthy body and a high IQ, to loving parents with a good income in an advanced and affluent society, so that all the riches of human culture are open to one who then has considerable freedom to choose his or her own mode of life. Another is born with a crippled body and a low IQ,

to unloving, unaffluent, and uncultured parents in a society in which that person is highly likely to become a criminal and to die an early and violent death. Is it fair that they should be born with such unequal advantages? If a new soul is created whenever a new baby is conceived, can the Creator who is responsible for each soul's unequal endowment be described as loving? We have all heard the story of John Bradford, who saw a criminal being taken to be hung and said, 'But for the grace of God there goes John Bradford.' The story is edifying insofar as it reminds us of God's grace to John Bradford; but what about God's grace, or lack of grace, to the condemned criminal? The more one contemplates the gross inequalities of human birth, and our western religious assumption that human beings are divinely created in these different conditions, the more one is likely to see grave injustices here.[11]

III

To what extent are these difficulties *really* removed by the doctrine of karma and reincarnation? For it is claimed that they are. Indeed:

> The alternative assumption of the Indian religions is that we have all lived before and that the conditions of our present life are a direct consequence of our previous lives. There is no arbitrariness, no randomness, no injustice in the inequalities of our human lot, but only cause and effect, the reaping now of what we have ourselves sown in the past. Our essential self continues from life to life, being repeatedly reborn or reincarnated, the state of its karma determining the circumstances of its next life.[12]

Let us examine the popular concept of the doctrine first. According to the popular concept there is a self which transmigrates from body to body. The philosophical problem which arises is: how do we know it is the same self or person? What are the criteria of our identity and can they be applied in this case? Now Hick identifies 'three strands of continuity that constitute what we normally mean by the identity of a human individual through time'. The first is memory, the second bodily continuity and the third is a pattern of mental dispositions. Hick argues that these criteria of identity are not met in the case of the popular concept because there is no memory of past life, so there goes one thread; and there is no bodily connection so there goes another thread. As for the third, personality types are so vague that they render firm identification impossible.

> There can be general similarities of character, found in such qualities as selfishness and unselfishness, introverted or extroverted types of personality, artistic or practical bents and in level of intelligence, let us say, between a male Tibetan peasant of the twelfth century BC and a female American college graduate of the twentieth century AD. However, such general similarities would *never by themselves* lead or entitle us to identify the two as the same person [my italics].[13]

Not 'by themselves' is important because it is the only thread of identification one is left with, and 'this criterion of character similarity is far too broad and permissive'.[14]

The difficulties Hick has pointed out are quite genuine. However it must be borne in mind that memories of past lives have been claimed and verified. In those particular cases, then, one criterion has been met. Again in other cases not only memories have been identified but physical marks on sites of physical injuries sustained in past lives have been located. Finally startling character traits have also been identified. One may refer here to the documented cases of Win Win Nyunt[15] in Burma and of Swarnalatā in India[16] and Marta Lorenz in Brazil.[17] One must not overlook the fact that

> this difficulty of not having an absolutely identical entity throughout affects not only the concept of the same person being reborn in different lives, it also affects any one life (that which is normally recognised as one life). The Bhāgavata Purāṇa was already aware of this problem: 'Like the flame of a lamp or the current of a river, the bodies of creatures, with the imperceptible passing of time, are in constant motion. Hence they are in a sense continually born and continually dying. Is the flame of the lamp one and the same as before? Is the current of water one and the same always? Is man, if identified with the body, the same man today that he was yesterday?' Mr. X himself is the same person throughout his present life only in the sense of being a

causally continuous series of states and events, for nothing in him remains identically the same from birth to death.[18]

One could further argue here that memory even within one life can have gaps so that memory cannot provide in that sense an iron-clad case for identity.[19] It could be argued, however, that visible bodily continuity by itself, or in combination with memory does endow one life with a measure of continuity which is difficult to establish across lives. But this continuity is physiological rather than logical for both the mind and body keep undergoing changes of various kinds.

It seems that the real difficulty with the popular concept is not so much with the criteria of identity as with some other factors. The first of these is logical. Can we infer from the fact that a *few* have been reborn (on solid evidence) that *all* are reborn? The second of these is psychological. Can the third criterion of psychological profile be really depended upon in view of the dynamic nature of human personality? Don't people change? Don't they change all the more between two distant points in time? And don't they change even more when their physical environment is altered? Have we not heard of the anthropologist who turned native?

Attention may now be directed to the Vedantic conception of the doctrine.

The Vedantic concept of karma and rebirth involves the doctrine of the three bodies or *śárīras*. According to the Vedānta, although we regard ourselves as a single entity we are really three distinct entities or bodies collapsed in one. Just as water appears as a single substance to the eye but when analysed chemically turns out really to consist of two substances – the gases hydrogen and oxygen (H_2O) in this case; similarly, although the individual appears as a single being to the eye, when analysed metaphysically, he turns out to be a case of three-in-one: three bodies collapsed in one. These are called the gross, the subtle and the causal bodies, the word 'body' being used to signify distinctness rather than corporeality' as in its usual sense, except in the first case. From the Vedantic viewpoint, the subtle and causal bodies, whom we may collectively call the 'soul', leave the gross body at the time of death and go on to inhabit another body in accordance with karma.

After presenting a more detailed account of the above Hick remarks:

If we ask why Hindus believe that this is a true account of the facts of human existence, there are three interlocking answers. One is that it is a revealed truth taught in the Vedas. A second is that reincarnation is a hypothesis that makes sense of many aspects of human life, including the inequalities of human birth; I shall return to this presently. The third is that there are the fragmentary memories of former lives to which we have already referred and also, even more important, the much fuller memories that are attained by those who have achieved *mokṣa*, liberation and enlightenment. It is claimed that the yogi, when he attains, remembers all his former lives and sees for himself the karmic connection that runs through a succession of apparently different and unrelated lives. This last item is for many in India the most important of all grounds for belief in reincarnation.[20]

Now each of the three answers need to be examined carefully, the last two more closely than the first as, in a discussion involving philosophy rather than religion, little weight may be attached to scriptural authority. But that too shall be examined in due course.

Hick does not regard the second answer as satisfactory because according to the Hindus there 'is no first life but a beginningless regress of incarnations', namely, that karma is *anādi*. Now as he points out 'one may affirm the beginningless character of the soul's existence in this way, but one cannot then claim that it renders either intelligible or morally acceptable the inequalities found in our human lot'.[21] The argument has some force but perhaps not as much as might appear at first sight. Let us suppose that in this life I happen to be rich but am caught practising financial fraud and am reduced to penury. My relative impoverishment, both in relation to my previous state and the present state of others, is thus the result of my karma. Now let us suppose that I was not caught and that as a result of the working, not of judicial, but of moral law, I was reduced to poverty in my next life. Now has karma not satisfactorily explained my situation? It is when we ask the question, not *when* did I steal, but *why* did I steal, that we open a can of worms. But one can see at once how, even in this life, a question such as *why* did I steal will lead to an infinite regress. Did I inherit the tendency or was it the result of my environment? If I inherited it how far back in my ancestry am I supposed to go? If it is the result of the environment, how far do we push the point? – to the slums of the industrial revolution? to the ghettos of medieval Europe? How far back in time do we travel? To give another example. I fall sick and ask a doctor for an explanation; he tells me I have caught a virus; just as I might go to a Hindu thinker and ask him why I have failed in business and he tells me it is the bad result of evil financial practices pursued in past lives. Now I return, apparently satisfied with the doctor's answer, but, suppose I begin to ask: where did the virus come from? Which earlier virus did it mutate from? One would be getting back to the distinction in evolution between organic and inorganic life. In other words, if not correctly understood, the idea of beginninglessness can easily become a red herring.

Hick also tries the other assumption, that of postulating 'a first life (as Hinduism does not)'[22] and shows how this leads to a dilemma: if the creatures were differently endowed there is no equality and if they were and the differences are environmentally caused then again God cannot escape that responsibility. A modern Hindu thinker who accepts the idea of an original creation has implied however that identically endowed souls in an identical environment may act differently, if they were given genuine free will by God, by the very genuineness of the free will.[23]

We turn now to the third answer given by the Hindus: that it is possible to recall past lives. Hick here raises two interesting points: (a) 'What exactly does reincarnation mean when it is thus given factual anchorage by a claimed retrospective Yogic memory of a series of lives that were not linked by memory while they were being lived?' and (b) that if a person rises to a level of such transcendental vision as to behold the succession of his own lives surely he can do the same with the lives of others so that not just his own but '*all* human lives, however different from their own several points of view, would be connected via a higher consciousness in the way postulated by the idea of reincarnation'.[24]

The first criticism relates to the role of a life of which one is not aware when one is leading another life and whose memory is subsequently retrieved. The implication seems to be that it is of little consequence. However, it seems that the word memory here should be qualified by the word *conscious*. As we know from modern psychoanalysis, the fact that we have forgotten some events does not mean that they have ceased to influence our psyche. It is clear, therefore, that from an empirical point of view the *fact* of past lives, even if the memory is lost, could continue to exert influence on later lives. Indeed just as forgotten facts are dredged up in psychoanalysis, forgotten lives are recalled by Yogis as a part of a similar therapeutic process: in the former case, for securing release from complexes; in the latter, for securing release from *saṁsāra*. A more important point now emerges as the embodied soul reaches this meta-empirical level. Hick points out that 'this higher state of consciousness did not experience those earlier lives and therefore it cannot in any ordinary sense be said to remember them. Rather, it is in a state *as though* it had experienced it, although in fact it did not.'[25] Let us consider here the example of going to a tragic movie. Did I experience the tragedy of the movie? As a movie-goer I experienced it, but I did not experience it in my life as such. Well then, did I experience it? Moreover did even the actor really experience it? I can recall the experience in whatever sense I may be said to have experienced it. The Yogi can similarly recall the lives as he went through them (as I saw the movie) in whatever sense they may be said to have been experienced.

The second criticism remains to be discussed. It is true that in a supernormal state of consciousness all channels are opened – to one's own past life *and* the lives of others. But this does *not* mean that either the Yogi confuses the two or we should. The Yogasūtra concerned, in this context, is III.18: Saṁskārasākṣātkaraṇāt pūrvajātijñānam. It is translated by James Haugthon Woods thus: 'As a result of direct-perception of subliminal-impressions there is (intuitive) knowledge of previous births'.[26] It should be clearly noted that the gloss by Vyāsa makes a clear distinction between recalling one's own past lives and those of others. Part of it runs: 'Precisely as in other cases there is also, as a result of the direct-perception of subliminal-impressions, a consciousness (*saṁvedana*) of the births of others.'[27] In other words, at this Yogic eschatological banquet, no Indian curry, in the form of a pot-pourri of the indiscriminate memories of the past lives of all, is served.

One may now revert to the question of scriptural authority. As mentioned earlier, from the point of view of the philosophy of religion, the point need not be considered seriously. But what we should consider is the following comment by Karl Potter, which is being cited in extenso in view of its appeal to positivism rather than scripturalism.

> Although scientifically minded (most Western) critics have tended to view the accounts reviewed above as either very poor

theories or else as myths or models themselves, it seems to me clear from the care with which the accounts are presented that their authors intended them quite literally as theories. Furthermore, it is not at all clear to me that they are any worse off with respect to the kinds of criticisms of theories sketched earlier than are theories deemed successful in Western science. The major criticism of the karma theory is that it is untestable, but similar criticisms can be made of theories in physics, for example those affected by the exigencies of quantum jumps or those which come under the restrictions suggested by Heisenberg's indeterminacy principle. Defenders of the theories in question respond that these difficulties are technical or technological, that in principle the theories are testable at least within broad limits. But surely the same can be said of the karma theory. It is not in principle untestable though in practice it is because of technical difficulties. The difficulties arise from our inability to determine with precision which person now alive inherits which past person's karmic residues. If one complains that it is precisely the responsibility of the karma theories to convince us that rebirth takes place at all, that there *are* any karmic residues, the parallel complaint may be recorded against the physicist who postulates unobservable microparticles. In both cases it is clear enough that what is to be explained is observable; in both cases the explanation involves postulation of unobservables. Technological advances may in time make possible testing of both types of theories – we may build bigger and better microscopes, or find theoretical ways of controlling the effects of quantum jumps or indeterminacy, and likewise we may eventually discover ways of identifying karmic residues and *vāsanās* and so of re-identifying them in another body at a later time.[28]

A third interpretation of karma and reincarnation as presented by Hick remains to be considered – the demythologised one. It is associated with the name of J. C. Jennings.[29] From this standpoint the idea of karma is regarded as 'a mythological expression of the fact that all our actions have effects upon some part of human community and have to be borne, for good or ill, by others in the future'.[30] Jennings makes the following points about the Buddha in relation to the doctrine of karma: (a) that he interpreted the idea of actions producing effects not from one life to another of the same individual because he did not believe in a permanent self but from one generation to another; and (b) that he treated life as an organic unity and thus preached collective karma.[31]

From this point onwards the discussion will be carried on historically and philosophically, in that order.

Historically both of the above points are difficult to sustain. Although it is true that the Buddha, according to the Theravāda tradition, preached the doctrine of Anatta or the absence of a permanent substratum which may be called the *ātman* in the individual, he never denied that it was the 'same changing entity' which underwent the results of the actions which were performed by it. This point has been securely established by modern scholarship.[32] But, just as the Buddha saw no permanent substratum in the individual, he saw none in the cosmos either, so that the idea of the whole world as other than an entity in flux[33] is difficult to support. There is some germ of truth in the suggestion that the idea of group karma may have been on its way towards appearing in Theravāda Buddhism, but that is about all that can be said.[34] Another historical objection would be that the concept of group karma is not unknown to Hinduism as such.[35]

Philosophically two points need to be distinguished. On the one hand Hick regards this demythologised expression of karma as 'a moral truth, a teaching of universal human responsibility',[36] perhaps one opposed to the war of all against all. On the other hand, according to Hick, 'both the more popular idea of the transmigration of souls and the more philosophical idea of the continuity of a 'subtle body' from individual to individual in succeeding generations can be seen as mythological expressions of this great moral truth'.[37]

Although one can easily share the sentiment that the reincarnation doctrine may be 'a vivid affirmation of human unity', it is not meant to be that. Human unity is affirmed in Hindu thought quite vividly[38] but it is a human individuality which is affirmed in the context of karma.[39] It seems best at this stage of the game to keep as open a mind on the reality or otherwise of karma and reincarnation, as on the question of the existence of God.

Notes and References

1. Ainslie T. Embree (ed.), *Alberuni's India* (New York: W. W. Norton, 1971) p. 50.

2. The Śaiva sect of Liṅgāyatas for instance rejected it. The Indian materialists rejected it as well, but were regarded as heterodox not because they rejected rebirth, but rather belief in Vedic authority.
3. Buddhism accepts karma but rejects reincarnation in the sense of a soul being reborn, see Surendranath Dasgupta, *A History of Indian Philosophy*, vol. I (Cambridge University Press, 1922) pp. 74, 75.
4. Jainism accepts karma and reincarnation but regards karma as a fine material substance which adheres to the soul, whereas in Hinduism karma operates as a principle and not as a substance. Surendranath Dasgupta, *A History of Indian Philosophy*, vol. I, pp. 73–4.
5. Sarvepalli Radhakrishnan and Charles A. Moore (eds.), *A Source Book of Indian Philosophy* (Princeton, New Jersey: Princeton University Press, 1971) p. xxix.
6. R. C. Zaehner (ed.), *The Concise Encyclopaedia of Living Faiths* (Boston: Beacon Press, 1959) pp. 416–17.
7. See for example Wendy Doniger O'Flaherty, *Karma and Rebirth in Classical Indian Traditions* (Berkeley: University of California Press, 1980); Charles F. Keyes and E. Valentine Daniel, *Karma: An Anthropological Inquiry* (Berkeley: University of California Press, 1983); and other works.
8. John H. Hick, *Philosophy of Religion*, 3rd edn. (Englewood Cliffs, New Jersey: Prentice-Hall, 1983) ch. 10.
9. Surendranath Dasgupta, *A History of Indian Philosophy* vol. I, p. 71. The choice of the word 'suffer' in the last line is unfortunate; 'undergo' would seem preferable as the results could be good and may not necessarily involve 'suffering' as the word seems to suggest.
10. Wendy Doniger O'Flaherty (ed.), *Karma and Rebirth in Classical Indian Traditions*, p. xi.
11. John H. Hick, op. cit., pp. 133–4.
12. Ibid., p. 134.
13. John H. Hick, op. cit., p. 137.
14. Ibid.
15. Francis Story, *Rebirth as Doctrine and Experience*, vol. II (Kandy: Buddhist Publication Society, 1975) p. 176.
16. Ian Stevenson, *Twenty Cases Suggestive of Reincarnation* (Charlottesville: University Press of Virginia, 1974) p. 82ff.
17. Ibid., p. 183ff.
18. Pratima Bowes, *The Hindu Religious Tradition: A Philosophical Approach* (London: Routledge & Kegan Paul, 1977) p. 60.
19. Ibid., pp. 61–2.
20. John H. Hick, op. cit., pp. 140–41.
21. Ibid.
22. Ibid., p. 142
23. This is how, it seems, the views of Dayānanda Sarasvatī (1824–1883) will have to be interpreted at one stage in his life; see J.T.F. Jordens, *Dayānanda Sarasvatī* (Delhi: Oxford University Press, 1979) p. 109. He subsequently reverted to the standard Hindu view of beginningless creation.
24. John H. Hick, op. cit., p. 141.

25. Ibid., p. 141.
26. James Haughton Woods (tr.), *The Yoga-System of Patañjali* (Cambridge, Mass.: Harvard University Press, 1914) p. 247.
27. Ibid.
28. Wendy Doniger O'Flaherty (ed.), op. cit., pp. 259–60.
29. It is developed by J. C. Jennings in *The Vedantic Buddhism of the Buddha* (London: Oxford University Press, 1948).
30. John H. Hick, *Philosophy of Religion*, p. 142.
31. Ibid., pp. 142–3.
32. Walpola Rahula, *What the Buddha Taught* (New York: Grove Press, 1974) p. 33ff.
33. Ibid., pp. 51, 52; also see Charles A. Moore (ed.), *The Indian Mind* (Honolulu: East-West Center Press, 1967) p. 74.
34. James P. McDermott, 'Is There Group Karma in Theravāda Buddhism?' *Numen* 23 (1976), pp. 67–80.
35. Wendy Doniger O'Flaherty (ed.), op. cit., p. 114, etc.
36. John H. Hick, op. cit., p. 143.
37. Ibid., p. 143
38. Charles A. Moore (ed.), *The Indian Mind*, p. 243. The *nṛsūkta* of the AtharvaVeda may also be referred to here, in which 'the object of adoration is not God but man' (K. M. Sen, *Hinduism* [Baltimore: Penguin Books, 1965] p. 46). Also see Troy Wilson Organ, *Hinduism: Its Historical Development* (New York, Woodbury: Barron's Educational Series, 1974) p. 34.
39. Ibid., p. 364.

9

The Truth-Claims of Different Religions

I

RELIGIOUS PLURALISM

The existence of a variety of religions on the surface of the globe has been an historical fact for a long time;[1] in our times it has become an existential fact. It has been called 'a new day in religious encounter'[2] when 'almost any faith from anywhere is a presence and an option throughout the world'.[3] John H. Hick has noticed the uniqueness of this situation in a global context[4] but it should be pointed out that the Indian situation has been religiously plural for a long time. 'The Hindu thinkers reckoned with the striking fact that men and women dwelling in India belonged to different communities, worshipped different gods, and practised different rites.'[5] Heinrich Zimmer commences his book on the philosophies of India with the striking statement that 'We of the Occident are about to arrive at a crossroads that was reached by the thinkers of India some seven hundred years before Christ.'[6] The statement sounds somewhat exaggerated but one should not on the other hand underestimate the extent and degree of religious ferment North India was undergoing at the time – a time in which virtually every shade of religious and philosophic opinion was represented.[7] One Buddhist text refers to sixty-two metaphysical views which were current.[8]

All this would serve to suggest that Indian thought may have interesting viewpoints to offer on the question of conflicting truth-claims on account of its long first-hand familiarity with such a situation. It is true nevertheless that religious pluralism as it is experienced by the modern world is global in scale while it has, by comparison, been local in India. It also now involves many more religious traditions than were involved in the Indian situation.

II

THE PHILOSOPHICAL SIGNIFICANCE OF RELIGIOUS PLURALISM

The philosophical significance of religious pluralism manifests itself at two levels. So long as the religions of the world developed in relative isolation the question of their conflicting truth-claims was not very pressing, but over the last few centuries

> the scholarly study of world religions has made possible an accurate appreciation of the faiths of other people and so has brought home to an increasing number of us the problem of the conflicting truth claims made by different religious traditions. This issue now emerges as a major topic demanding a prominent place on the agenda of the philosopher of religion.[9]

Apart from the fact that religious pluralism adds a new dimension to the agenda of the philosopher of religion, it also raises several major issues. In this respect, philosophy of religion takes its cue from Hume 'that, in matters of religion, whatever is different is contrary; and that it is impossible the religions of ancient Rome, of Turkey, of Siam, and of China should, all of them, be established on any solid foundation'.[10] Hume further considers an individual item such as miracles, and remarks:

> Every miracle, therefore, pretended to have been wrought in any of these religions (and all of them abound in miracles), as its direct scope is to establish the particular religion to which it is attributed; so has it the same force, though more indirectly, to overthrow every other system.[11]

The same could be said of scriptures, or rituals, or myths. One could generalise the point so that, Hick argues,

> By the same reasoning, any ground for believing a particular religion to be true must operate as a ground for believing every other religion to be false; accordingly, for any particular religion there will always be far more reason for believing it to be false than for believing it to be true. This is the skeptical argument

> that arises from the conflicting truth claims of the various world faiths.[12]

The Hindu view on the matter, at least in our own times, is diametrically opposed to the one just stated. The philosophical grounds for this difference will be discussed later. At this stage a statement of the Hindu position must suffice. It is made by S. Radhakrishnan. The length of the quotation requires no apology on account of its relevance, representing as it does the view of a major spokesman of neo-Hinduism.

> The Hindu accepts all genuine formulations of the supreme adventures, all names given to the supreme reality. He believes that every creed that helps to ennoble and sanctify human living is justified. Our doctrinal expressions are partial visions of supreme reality and our codes of conduct are imperfect attempts to organize human life in accordance with the supreme end. Whatever dogma we may start from, whatever approach we may adopt, if we persist in our endeavour, we shall reach the truth behind the dogmas. Nobody possesses the truth, we are all seeking for it. The Hindu has no sympathy with nationalism in religion. He stands for an appreciation of other religions and thus serves the reconciliation of mankind. Even as the brotherhood of mankind is quite consistent with the retention of separate national loyalties so long as the latter are held subordinate to the common weal of mankind, so Hinduism believes that the ultimate achievement of unity in religion can be attained by preserving and purifying the different historical faiths. To-day Hinduism is confronted by the missionary religions of Islam and Christianity, which claim that their revelations contain the full and only self-disclosure of God. The universality they aim at is capable of achievement only if the other religions lose their individuality. Hinduism, however, by virtue of its historical circumstances, does not lay claim to any exclusive possession of truth and is aware that societies not inferior to its own in intelligence and virtue adopt views of the unseen world which are apparently different from its own.[13]

III

WESTERN APPROACHES TO RELIGIOUS PLURALISM: ANALYSIS OF THE VIEWS OF W. A. CHRISTIAN, W. C. SMITH AND JOHN H. HICK

One of the scholars who has addressed himself to the issue is W. A. Christian.[14] He may be seen as starting from the existential situation that in life there are questions to which we know the answers and questions to which we do not. It is only in the latter case that beliefs arise, as, in the former, facts settle the issue.

Christian develops the idea of a proposal for belief. Let us consider one which has been a point of contention between Jews and Christians, that Jesus is the Messiah. There is a conflict here to begin with in the sense that for the Jews the Messiah is to come and for the Christians he has. The problem recedes however if we ask what each group means by the term Messiah. If for the Christians the Messiah is a divine saviour, but for the Jews the restorer of Israel, then although the same word is being used the connotations are so distinct as to avoid conflict. However, the problem reappears if we speak of the Messiah as 'the one whom God promised to send to redeem Israel', and now identify Jesus with the Messiah. At this point the Christians accept the belief proposal but the Jews reject it. Differences can be seen as arising not only between traditions but among groups of traditions. The following four statements may be considered:

(A) Jesus is the Messiah;
(B) Jesus is the one whom God promised to send to redeem Israel;
(C) There is a being who rules the world who acts in history who sent Jesus, as the one whom God promised to send to redeem Israel who is the Messiah;
(D) The source of all beings rules the world who acts in history who sent Jesus as the one whom God promised to send to redeem Israel who is the Messiah.

(A) is acceptable to both Christians and Jews; (B) not to Jews; (C) neither to Stoics nor Jews; (D) neither to Stoics, Jews nor Monist Hindus. This is one way in which doctrinal disagreements could ramify. These Christian distinguishes from what he calls 'basic religious disagreements' in which 'different subjects are assigned to the same predicate'.

Predicate	Subject
Ground of being	God (theist)
	Nature (pantheist)
Supreme goal of life	Beatific vision (Christianity)
	Nirvāṇa (Buddhism)
That on which we unconditionally depend	Allah (Islam)
	God (Christianity)
Ultimate	Brahman (Hinduism)
	Truth (Humanism)

Thus both of these – 'doctrinal disagreements' and 'basic religious disagreements' exist among religions, and cannot be avoided by treating each religion as a 'language-game'.[15]

A Hindu response to the existence of both 'doctrinal disagreements' and 'basic religious disagreements' would be: though differences are indeed involved, they need not be considered disagreements. In these matters Hindu thought tends to extend the approach it adopts towards differences which exist *within* its various schools and sects, towards differences among religious traditions in general. One could well raise the question whether such an extension is legitimate, for different sects and schools of philosophy within Hinduism may share a common ground which the different religious traditions may not. Most Hindu thinkers seem convinced that the same body of general principles is applicable to differences both within Hinduism and among the various religions. To see how this principle operates one may first look at the differences within the Hindu religious tradition. There are the six schools of philosophy which differ among themselves and have been engaged in debating with each other for centuries.[16] One consideration serves to add even more force to this statement, that while in the history of Western philosophy the different schools of thought come into existence successively, in India the different schools of thought 'though not originating simultaneously, flourish together during many centuries, and pursue parallel courses of growth'[17] generating an atmosphere of continuous debate. Apart from the various schools of philosophy, the Hindu religious tradition is also internally differentiated by the existence of sects – the most prominent being the Vaiṣṇava and the Śaiva sects who differ among themselves.[18] More recently the modern period of Indian history has been distinguished by the emergence of numerous reform movements which also differ among themselves.[19] Thus differences within itself are as much a part, *perhaps a greater part*, of Hinduism as of any other religious tradition. What then has been the Hindu approach to these differences within itself? We shall confine ourselves here to the philosophical aspects of the question. After all the debating among the various schools of Hindu philosophy (which still continues), Vijñañabhikṣu, who lived in the second half of the sixteenth century AD, developed the view that 'all the orthodox systems of Indian philosophy (of which Sāṅkhya and Yoga are two) contain the highest truth, though leading to it from diverse and apparently antagonistic starting points'.[20] The idea of different starting points reflects the Hindu idea of *prasthānabheda*, a term which denotes different points of departure (as distinguished from the presumptive unity of destination).

The movement at the level of schools of philosophy thus has been in the direction of reconciliation and mutual recognition despite the differences, which are regarded as apparent, or secondary, or explicable in terms of different starting points or differing capacities.[21] A similar movement underlies the approach to sectarian, as distinguished from philosophical, differences within the Hindu religious tradition. Though the two main streams of Vaiṣṇava and Śaiva devotion have sometimes produced eddies of conflict when they have met, by and large they have flowed alongside smoothly.[22] A tendency to show Viṣṇu and Śiva, the 'two great divine powers, as complementary' is much in evidence.

> The two deities – 'the two highest who are one' – may even be invoked under the joint title Pradyumna–Īśvara, that is Hari-Hara, a figure which – whatever inspiration sculptors might derive from it to express the coincidence of opposites mutually supporting each other – never rose to real importance in religious praxis. Both gods are sometimes praised as being, each of them, one half of the highest God, or the original form of God is said to be composed of two 'halves' known individually as Śiva and Viṣṇu. In illustration of the difference in attitude between a mystic and a philosopher belonging to the same Viṣṇuite tradition I may recall that, whereas the saint and poet Nammālvār

> saw no difference in a so-called sectarian mark on the forehead made with sacred dust and one made, in the Śivaite way, with ashes, the philosopher Vedāntadeśika preferred to interpret in the poet's work the word for 'ashes' to mean the dust under Viṣṇu's feet in order to avoid any thought of ashes.[23]

Vedantadeśika was a sectarian or Vaiṣṇava philosopher. It is to a scholar philosophising about Hinduism in general, in such a way as takes into account both elements of philosophical and sectarian divisions within Hinduism, we now turn to tie the foregoing discussions back into W. A. Christian's analysis. Pratima Bowes identifies four strands in Hinduism: (a) non-dualistic; (b) polytheistic; (c) monotheistic (qualified) and (d) self-realisation of spirit.[24] The first two categories are fairly straightforward; the third does *not* refer to Rāmānuja's system, but to the fact that Hindu theism is directed to a particular god or goddess – Viṣṇu, Śiva and so on – and is in this sense qualified. The fourth category refers to the Sāṅkhya-Yoga type of spirituality. Bowes now makes the point that these descriptions are to be taken tentatively and not substantively in the sense that it is not a question of whether the ultimate reality is this or that, but rather that the same reality may be treated one way or the other. It is a matter of 'language'; the question 'is not whether there is only one God or many gods, but what language – of God or gods – fits 'a particular 'context of viewing the divine'.[25] Bowes goes on to say:

> We have seen that religious language in the Hindu tradition is not of one kind but many, polytheistic, monistic or non-dualistic, monotheistic (qualified), and even that of self-realisation as spirit (the language of Samkhya-yoga). They do not all say the same thing about religious reality and yet all these are accepted as valid explorations of this reality by most Hindus. This is why I have used the term 'religious reality' rather than 'God,' as the intended objective reference of all these languages, since 'God' fits only one kind of language, the monotheistic.[26]

From this it is but a step to the position that *Hinduism uses the kind of language-game in which 'doctrinal disagreements' and 'basic religious disagreements'* are accommodated with relative ease when compared with the 'languages' used by other traditions. This seems to be the clear implication of the following statement of Bowes when applied to the discussion on hand:

A philosopher can only examine the language that is used in respect of a domain to see what is involved in the use of his language, including the language of truth used as both ontological and epistemological categories, and I shall confine my investigations to this. In the Hindu tradition, while Truth, in the sense of the Being of religious reality, is said to be absolute, truth in the sense of the epistemological status of the statements we make about it is not claimed to be so, so it is not the case that only one statement about it can be accepted as true while others must be rejected as false.[27]

The views of W. C. Smith on the question of conflicting truth-claims may now be examined.[28] W. C. Smith argues that what 'we call a religion – an empirical entity that can be traced historically and mapped geographically – is a human phenomenon. Christianity, Hinduism, Judaism, Buddhism, Islam, and so on are human creations whose history is part of the wider history of human culture'.[29] To quote Smith himself now:

> It is a surprisingly modern aberration for anyone to think that Christianity is true or that Islam is – since the Enlightenment, basically, when Europe began to postulate religions as intellectualistic systems, patterns of doctrine, so that they could for the first time be labeled 'Christianity' and 'Buddhism,' and could be called true or false.[30]

The issue of conflicting truth-claims on this view has a historical dimension to it which we overlook at our peril by treating it as a purely philosophical issue.

This is the first point, that the reification of 'religion' is a recent historical phenomenon. Now when we turn to the other end of the scale and look at the origins of various religions, Smith argues that the credal and institutional structure of a religion 'stands in a questionable relationship to that original event or idea'[31] which gave rise to it. This second point may be dramatised by stating, for instance, that Christ did not preach to Christians but to all human beings. Religion thus, in this sense, is a human phenomenon.[32]

A third point is: each religion is so closely involved with a culture that 'it is not appropriate to speak of a religion as being true or false, any more than it is to speak of a civilization as being true or false'.[33]

The Hindu response to this position could be manifold but may be confined to three points. Firstly W. C. Smith's argument is essentially historical in nature. He states that the reification of the idea of religion is a recent historical development; his discussion of the origins of religion is also historical in nature. The blending of religion and culture can also be regarded primarily as a historical process. By contrast Hindu thought as such does not set much store by history:

> One of the characteristics of ancient Hindu thought is its indifference to history. In discussing the contents of a book, for instance, ancient and even medieval Indian writers care very little for the date or the life of the author. They care more for the truth of experience or the soundness of doctrine than for the circumstances that gave it birth. What Sir Charles Eliot says of the religious mind in general is particularly applicable to them. 'The truly religious mind does not care for the history of religion, just as, among us, the scientific mind does not dwell on the history of science.' But there is no doubt that the Hindu writers went to one extreme in ignoring history altogether while modern Western writers go to the other extreme in making too much of the historical treatment of thought and art and digging at the roots of a tree instead of enjoying its flower and fruit.[34]

Thus from the Hindu point of view, a position on the conflicting truth-claims of religions which bases itself on history has inherent limitations, if religious truth as such is regarded as transhistorical. This should not be taken to imply that the historical factor is totally disregarded; rather it confirms the Hindu viewpoint instead of providing a fresh standpoint. Pratima Bowes considers historical along with other factors as determining the apprehension of religious reality:

> All these formulations of religious reality apparently contradict one another, but, . . . if we become aware that they are approaching religious reality from different perspectives and with different purposes in view we shall find that there is in reality no contradiction. Rather they are complementary views none of which can claim exclusive or absolute validity, although each one has validity in reality to its own point of view. *There may be historical reasons* why a certain purpose or framework of approach is adopted by a religious community at a certain time,

> with its appropriate practice for effecting integration. That is, a certain approach may serve the felt religious needs of a community better than others at a certain time.[35]

Modern Hindu thinkers would tend to agree with Smith that religion is a human phenomenon, but again their understanding would tend to differ, as will become clear when we resume citing Pratima Bowes:

> Also there may be psychological reasons (intellectual and emotional) why an individual may prefer a certain approach to another, both of which are available to him. But from the point of view of philosophy all one can do is to bring out the logic involved in each form and show how the truth it claims is relative to its purpose. But this kind of understanding of religious truth is possible only if it is accepted that this truth is a human truth, that is, attained by the human mind in its search after religious reality and not something that has been handed over from another source, beyond man. It is true that revelation is claimed by people in the Hindu tradition in respect of the Vedas and Upaniṣads, but the compatibility of these scriptures with every shade of religious opinion, as the history of the Hindu tradition shows, makes it clear that the truths of the Vedas were revealed to Vedic seers through their own search and their own capacity for religious experience, insight and illumination; they were not received from above.[36]

If truth is human in this sense, then it is relative to those who are apprehending it. The statement has an epistemological rather than a historical flavor when made in Hinduism. One should point out that Bowes is not quite correct in representing the concept of revelation in Hinduism the way she does (but it is difficult to be quite wrong in saying something about Hinduism either). The *standard* concept of revelation in Hinduism is not one of human truth.[37] It is, however, a view which finds support in the Sāṅkhya school[38] and among modern Hindu thinkers.[39]

That truth or falsity is not an appropriate question to ask of a religion is a view Hindu thinkers can easily relate to, as would be clear from the foregoing discussion. But at this point a vital distinction must be drawn between truth and truth-claim. A religion could be true and yet its truth-claim could be false. It could be said to be true in the sense that its believers held it to be true or belief in its truth-claims was pragmatically wholesome. It would be true in the sense that, as 'frameworks' of apprehending religious reality are many 'truths are said to be many'. But this does not mean that its truth-claims are thereby exempted from the application of critical philosophical procedures, as is clear from the vigour and rigour with which this was done by the different schools of thought within Hinduism.

Another scholar whose views may now be examined is John H. Hick.[40] He employs the Kantian distinction between the thing-in-itself (*ding an sich*) and the thing as apprehended and uses it to provide a philosophical framework for accommodating religious pluralism, by urging that we 'think in terms of a single divine noumenon and perhaps many diverse phenomena'.[41] He then identifies two fundamental ways in which the real-in-itself may be experienced – as the Absolute or God. As the Absolute it is then the impersonal religious reality as '*impersonae* experienced within the different strands of non-theistic religion' as 'Brahman, Nirvana, Sunyata, the Dharma, the Dharmakaya, the Tao'.[42] As God it is experienced as Yahweh, 'God', Allah, Kṛṣṇa.[43]

The reader will readily recognise that this is a common Hindu position.[44] Hick tries to distinguish his position, it would appear, from the Hindu Vedantic position by adding:

> It is characteristic of the more mystical forms of awareness of the Real that they seem to be direct, and not mediated – or therefore distorted – by the perceptual machinery of the human mind. However, our hypothesis will have to hold that even the apparently direct and unmediated awareness of the Real in the Hindu *moksha*, in the Buddhist *satori*, and in the unitive mysticism of the West, is still the conscious experience of human subject and as such is influenced by the interpretative set of the cognizing mind. All human beings have been influenced by the culture of which they are a part and have received, or have developed in their appropriation of it, certain deep interpretative tendencies which help to form their experience and are thus continually confirmed within it. We see evidence of such deep 'sets' at work when we observe that mystics formed by Hindu, Buddhist, Christian, Muslim, and Jewish religious cultures report distinctively different forms of experience. Thus, far from it being the case that they all undergo an identical experience but report it in

different religious languages, it seems more probable that they undergo characteristically different unitive experiences (even though with important common features), the differences being due to the conceptual frameworks and meditational disciplines supplied by the religious traditions in which they participate.

Thus it is a possible, and indeed an attractive, hypothesis – as an alternative to total skepticism – that the great religious traditions of the world represent different human perceptions of and response to the same infinite divine Reality.[45]

One of the Hindu positions with hoary ancestry has been that people who undergo religious experience, especially mystical religious experience, do not 'undergo an identical experience' but rather that they experience in different (or even similar ways) an *identical* reality. It is the reality which is identical, not the experience.[46] Once the Hindu position is thus clarified there remains little to distinguish Hick's position from it – except the use of Western philosophical terms. Ancient Hindu thought and modern Western philosophy of religion seem to converge on this single point, although the point, as in Euclidean geometry, has to be taken as given.

Notes and References

1. See Niels C. Nielsen, Jun., *et al.* (eds.), *Religions of the World* (New York: St Martin's Press, 1983).
2. Robert S. Ellwood, Jun., *An Introduction to the Religious Life of Mankind* (Englewood Cliffs, New Jersey: Prentice-Hall, 1976) p. 2.
3. Ibid., p. 2.
4. John H. Hick, *Philosophy of Religion*, 3rd edn (Englewood Cliffs, New Jersey: Prentice-Hall, 1983) p. 107.
5. S. Radhakrishnan, *The Hindu View of Life* (New York: Macmillan, 1927) p. 12.
6. Joseph Campbell (ed.), Heinrich Zimmer, *Philosophies of India* (New York: Meridian Books, 1964) p. 1.
7. See K. N. Jayatilleke, *Early Buddhist Theory of Knowledge* (London: George Allen & Unwin, 1963) Chs I–III; Wm Theodore de Bary, *Sources of Indian Tradition*, vol. I (New York: Columbia University Press, 1958) pp. 39–41; and other works.
8. David J. Kalupahana, *Buddhist Philosophy: A Historical Analysis* (Honolulu: The University Press of Hawaii, 1976) p. 155.
9. John H. Hick, op. cit., p. 107.
10. Cited in John H. Hick, op. cit., p. 108.
11. Ibid.

12. Ibid.
13. L. S. S. O'Malley (ed.), *Modern India and the West* (London: Oxford University Press, 1968 [first published 1941]) p. 343.
14. W. A. Christian, *Meaning and Truth in Religion* (Princeton, New Jersey: Princeton University Press, 1964).
15. This is a summarisation of W. A. Christian's analysis as presented by John H. Hick, op. cit., pp. 108–11.
16. See Ninian Smart, *Doctrine and Argument in Indian Philosophy* (London: George Allen & Unwin, 1964).
17. Satischandra Chatterjee and Dhirendramohan Datta, *An Introduction to Indian Philosophy* (University of Calcutta, 1968) p. 9.
18. See J. Gonda, *Viṣṇuism and Śivaism: A Comparison* (London: The Athlone Press, 1970).
19. J. N. Farquhar, *Modern Religious Movements in India* (Delhi: Munshiram Manoharlal, 1967 [first Indian edition]).
20. Joseph Campbell (ed.), op. cit., p. 291.
21. Satischandra Chatterjee and Dhirendramohan Datta, op. cit., pp. 11–12.
22. See J. Gonda, op. cit., ch. V.
23. Ibid., pp. 108–9.
24. Pratima Bowes, *The Hindu Religious Tradition* (London: Routledge & Kegan Paul, 1977) chs IV–VII.
25. Ibid., p. 104.
26. Ibid., p. 272.
27. Ibid.
28. Wilfred Cantwell Smith, *The Meaning and End of Religion* (New York: Macmillan, 1963).
29. John H. Hick, op. cit., p. 112.
30. Ibid.
31. Ibid., p. 113.
32. Wilfred Cantwell Smith, op. cit., pp. 128–9.
33. John H. Hick, op. cit., p. 113.
34. D. S. Sarma, *Hinduism Through the Ages* (Calcutta: Bharatiya Vidya Bhavan, 1956) p. 1.
35. Pratima Bowes, op. cit., p. 281.
36. Ibid., p. 281.
37. See K. Satchidananda Murty, *Revelation and Reason in Advaita Vedānta* (New York: Columbia University, 1959) pp. 238–9; M. Hiriyanna, *The Essentials of Indian Philosophy* (London: George Allen & Unwin, 1949) pp. 168–9, 209 fn. 13.
38. Satischandra Chatterjee and Dhirendramohan Datta, op. cit., p. 279.
39. T. M. P. Mahadevan, *Outlines of Hinduism* (Bombay: Chetana, 1971) pp. 28–9; and other works.
40. John H. Hick, *Philosophy of Religion*, pp. 118–21.
41. Ibid., p. 120.
42. Ibid.
43. Ibid.
44. See K. M. Sen, *Hinduism* (Baltimore: Penguin Books, 1961) pp. 21, 37, 39, 77, etc.

45. John H. Hick, op. cit., pp. 119–20.
46. S. Radhakrishnan, *Eastern Religions and Western Thought* (New York: Galaxy, 1959) pp. 318–19; Troy Wilson Organ, *The Hindu Quest for the Perfection of Man* (Athens, Ohio: Ohio University, 1970) pp. 73–4.

Glossary

Adhikaraṇa	A subdivision of the Brahma Sūtra dealing with a particular topic.
Advaita Vedānta	A system of Indian philosophy representing a form of Hindu absolutism, which received its classical formulation at the hands of Śaṅkara or Śaṁkara (*C.* 788–812).
Āḻvārs	Twelve canonized devotees of Viṣṇu in Tamilnadu generally believed to have flourished from seventh to tenth century AD.
Arthavāda	Scriptural material of an auxiliary nature, as distinguished from those parts containing its main support.
Bhāgavata Purāṇa	Perhaps the best known of the 18 Purāṇas (texts which deal with Hindu mythos in the broadest sense). It deals with the early life of Kṛṣṇa, an incarnation of Viṣṇu.
Brahman	The term used to denote the ultimate Reality in the school of Hindu philosophy known as Vedānta, as also within its numerous subdivisions.
Brahma Sūtra	An aphoristic condensation of the teachings of the Upaniṣads. It is also known as the Vedānta Sūtra.
Dvaita Vedānta	A system of Vedānta which offers a dualistic and theistic interpretation of the Upaniṣads, the quintessential philosophical texts of Hinduism. It received its classical formulation at the hands of Madhvācārya (1199–1278).

Gopī — A milkmaid of the region of Vraja, devotionally associated with Kṛṣṇa during the early phase of his life.

Guṇa — The word can mean both 'strand' or constituents such as that of a rope as well as a quality of disposition. The uses are not unconnected. In the sense of constituents it refers to the three components which compose, coexist and cohere in matter (*prakṛti*). They are (1) *sattva* (2) *rajas* and (3) *tamas*, representing the pure and the light; the kinetic or active; the static or inertial elements respectively. The corresponding adjectival forms are *sāttvika*, *rājasika* and *tāmasika*.

In the sense of quality the three terms respectively denote purity, volatility and stolidity of disposition as a component of personality.

Hindu Thought, Schools of — The schools of Hindu thought are formally enumerated as six, all sharing a concern with liberation (*mokṣa*) but each possessing primarily, though not exclusively, certain characteristic features. Thus *Nyāya* is characterised by logical realism; *Vaiśeṣika* by atomistic pluralism; *Sāṅkhya* by an atheistic dualism of matter and spirit; *Yoga* by a system of psychophysiological praxis; *Mīmāṁsā* by sacrificial ritualism and *Vedānta* by absolutism and/or theism. On account of philosophical affinity and alliance these systems are often hyphenated as *Nyāya-Vaiśeṣika*: the epistemology of Nyāya dovetailing with

	the ontology of Vaiśeṣika; *Sāṅkhya-Yoga*: the metaphysics of Sāṅkhya combining with the praxis of Yoga; and *Mīmāṁsā-Vedānta*: both accepting the Vedic revelation but differing as to its import. All are considered orthodox on account of their nominal acceptance of Vedic authority.
Kaivalya	The liberative state of splendid isolation of a spirit (*puruṣa*) from matter (*prakṛti*), once the spirit has succeeded in releasing itself from the bondage of matter.
Karma (or Karman)	The doctrine that actions – mental, verbal or physical – produce ineluctable consequences. The consequences are believed to be commensurate with the moral quality of the deed and may manifest themselves not just in one but through several lives.
Rajas (Rājasika)	See Guṇa.
Rāmanāma	The name of Rāma, used either for an incarnation of Viṣṇu in particular or as a name for God in general.
Rishis (or Ṛṣis)	The seers, men as well as women, to whom the hymns contained in the Vedas, the Hindu sacred books *par excellence*, were revealed.
Śāstra	Any body of literature in Hinduism as a whole possessing an authoritative character, inclusive of revelation (*śruti*) and tradition (*smṛti*).
Sattva (Sāttvika)	See Guṇa.

Saṁskāra	Psychic residue of past lives and deeds as constitutive of one's present personality in the form of latent predispositions.
Sāñkhya (or Sāṁkhya)	One of the six systems of Hindu philosophy, along with *nyāya, vaiśeṣika, yoga, mīmāṁsā* and *vedānta*.
Śaiva	A worshipper of or pertaining to Śiva.
Śiva	One of the two pre-eminent deities of Hindu devotion, along with Viṣṇu.
Śrāddha	A memorial service for the departed, invested with much social and ritual significance in Hinduism.
Śraddhā	An attitude of faith in what is revealed as truth.
Swami	A person in Hinduism, who, by undergoing a rite, has severed all formal bonds with society in quest of salvation; distinguished by the ochre colour of the robes worn and not to be confused with a priest.
Tāmas (Tāmasika)	See Guṇa.
Upādhi	A limiting adjunct or condition attached to an entity.
Vaiṣṇava	A worshipper of or pertaining to Viṣṇu.
Veda	The revealed scriptures of Hinduism.
Vedānta	The most influential form of Hindu thought in general, using the last section of the Vedas as its point of philosophical departure.

Viṣṇu	One of the two major gods, along with Śiva, towards whom devotion in Hinduism is primarily directed.
Viśiṣṭādvaita Vedānta	A system of Hindu philosophy representing a form of Hindu theism, which received its classical formulation at the hands of Rāmānuja (C. 1017–1137). The term is often translated as qualified non-dualism.
Vyūha	A development in Vaiṣṇava theology as distinguished from the Hindu in general, somewhat akin to the trinitarian formulation in Christianity, but involving a fourfold manifestation.

For Further Reading

Bowes, Pratima, *The Hindu Religious Tradition: A Philosophical Approach* (London: Routledge & Kegan Paul, 1977).

Deutsch, Eliot, *Advaita Vedānta: A Philosophical Reconstruction* (Honolulu: East-West Center Press, 1969).

Devaraja, N. K., *Hinduism and Christianity* (New Delhi: Asia Publishing House, 1969).

Devaraja, N. K., *Hinduism and the Modern Age* (New Delhi: Islam and the Modern Age Society, 1975).

Herman, Arthur L., *The Problem of Evil and Indian Thought* (Delhi: Molilal Banarsidass, 1976).

Hick, John H., *Death and Eternal Life* (London: Collins, 1976; Macmillan, 1985).

Hick, John H., *Evil and the God of Love* (London: Macmillan, 1977).

Hiriyanna, M., *Outlines of Indian Philosophy* (London: George Allen & Unwin, 1964 [first published 1932]).

Hiriyanna, M., *The Essentials of Indian Philosophy* (London: George Allen & Unwin, 1949).

Kumarappa, Bharatan, *The Hindu Conception of the Deity as Culminating in Rāmānuja* (London: Luzac, 1934).

Mahadevan, T. M. P., *Outlines of Hinduism* (Bombay: Chetana, 1971 [first published 1956]).

Satchidananda Murty, K., *Revelation and Reason in Advaita Vedānta* (New York: Columbia University, 1959).

Smart, Ninian, *Doctrine and Argument in Indian Philosophy* (London: George Allen Unwin, 1964).

Smart, Ninian, *The Yogi and the Devotee* (London: George Allen & Unwin, 1968).

Tripathi, R. K., *Problems of Philosophy and Religion* (Varanasi: Banaras Hindu University, 1971).

Index

Abhaṅgas, 75
Absolute, the, 162
Absolutistic schools, in Hinduism, 78, 82
  and language, 85
ādhibhautika, 48
ādhidaivika, 48
Adhikaraṇa, 75
Adhyātma Rāmāyaṇa, 50
ādhyātmika, 48
Adṛṣṭa, 2, 3
Advaita Vedānta, 15, 48, 49, 52, 55, 57, 59, 103, 104
  authority of Vedas in, 66
  God and *karma* in, 55–7
  ignorance and evil in, 55–6
  līlā in, 57
  and living liberation, 107
  origins of Vedas in, 64–5
  see also Śaṅkara
Advaitin, the, 64, 79, 86
Āgamas, 69, 70, 72
Agni, 24, 95
Agnihotra, 32
ākāśa, 9
Albiruni, 140
Allah, 156, 162
Āḻvārs, the, 75
aṁśa, 73
ānanda, 84
anādi, 145
analogical extension, 95
analogy, 101
anantam, 82, 84
Anselm, 8, 9, 10
anubhava, 15
anumāna, 101; *see also* inference
apauruṣeya, 64, 65, 69
āpta, 93
Aquinas, Thomas, 2, 3, 4, 9, 10, 80, 81, 82
  proofs for God's existence, 3–4
  compared with Udayana, 4
arcā, 72
archetype, 95, 96
  Jungian, 95
  Eliadean, 95
argument from destruction, 20–2
aseity, 9
Aśvamedha sacrifice, 34
atheism, 18, 87, 118, 119
  ethical, 22
atheistic hedonism, 127
atheists, 100, 101, 112, 113
Ātman, 133
Augustine, 47
authority of scripture, 13, 14, 15, 92
avatāra, 72
avidyā, 55, 56; *see also* ignorance

Bhagavadgītā, the, 63, 71, 97, 134, 137
Bhāgavata Purāṇa, 71, 143
bhakti-yoga, 110
Bhartṛhari, 85–6
Bible, the, 62, 63, 65, 66, 68, 81, 88, 92, 94, 116
bliks, 105, 106, 115
body, 124, 126, 127, 129, 130, 144; *see also śarīras*
body-soul relationship, 126
  Hebraic concept of, 126–7
  materialist concept of, 126–7
  spiritual concept of, 126
Bowes, Pratima, 95, 99, 158, 160, 161
Brahmā, 46, 85
Brahman, 13, 54, 56, 57, 65, 66, 75, 78, 79, 82, 83, 84, 86, 87, 88, 103, 104, 133, 156, 162
Brāhmaṇas, 33
brahmānubhava, 75
Brahmasūtra, 75
Bṛhadāraṇyaka, 74
Buddha, 16, 46
  and doctrine of *karma*, 148–9
Buddhism, 16, 21, 140, 152, 156, 159

and *dukkha*, 47
Theravāda, 149
Buddhists, 32, 41, 126
Bultmann, 116

Cabbalists, 93
Caitanya movement, 75, 108
Cārvākas, school of, 32
critique of religion in, 32–41
Freudian critique of religion in, 33–5
logical critique of God in, 35–41
Marxist critique of religion in, 32–5
see also materialism
caryā, 133
caste system, 133
causation, 39
Christian, W. A., 155, 156, 158
Christianity, 2, 16, 17, 63, 65, 68, 91, 92, 126, 133, 140, 155, 156, 159
incarnation in, 72–3
and science, 41–2
soul and identity in, 131
Christians, 65, 155
and hell, 135
Christian situation, 75
Christian thought, 62, 64, 94
lakṣaṇā in, 81
cit, 84
concomitance, 5–6, 38, 39
consciousness, 124, 125, 146, 147
arguments for autonomous character of, 127–8
cosmological argument, 11, 12–13, 15
and Śaivism, 21
creation, 54, 85
cyclical, 85
as demonstrative of God's glory, 54–5
as sport, 54–5
cumulative method, 82–5

damnation, eternal, 134
Darśana literature, 69, 70
Darwinism, 41
dāsa, 133
Descartes, René, 126
design argument; *see* teleological argument
destiny, 51
Deuteronomy, 66
Deutsch, Eliot, 104
Devadatta, 79
devil, the, 134
dharma, 93, 125
Dharma, the, 162
Dharmakāya, 162
Dharmaśāstras, 70
disagreement,
doctrinal, 155, 156, 158
basic religious, 156, 158
divya, 138
Divyaprabandham, 75
doctrine of *karma* and reincarnation, 140–9
absence of, in Western thought, 141–2
demythologised interpretation of, 141, 148–9
popular concept of, 141, 142–4
Vedantic concept of, 141, 144–8
dualism; *see* Dvaita Vedānta
Dvaita Vedānta, school of, 52, 59
critique of other schools, 59
God and *karma* in, 59

Eliade, Mircea, 109
Eliot, Sir Charles, 160
ethics, 91, 93, 141
evil, 135
and Brahman, in Viśiṣṭādvaita Vedānta, 58
concept of, 47–8
distinctions in, 47
and God, 46–7, 52: in Advaita Vedānta, 55–7; in Dvaita Vedānta, 59; in Nyāya, 52–5; in Viśiṣṭādvaita Vedānta, 57–8
in Hindu schools of thought, 48–9, 134
and ignorance, in Advaita Vedānta, 55–6
karma, as explanation for, 49–52
man, as a cause of, 50

problem of, 46–59, 103
as relational, 49
Existentialism, 116

faith, 62, 63, 64, 67, 68, 108, 133
as cognitive, 116
falsification, 98, 99, 102, 103, 104, 108, 111, 113, 114, 115
falsity, 93, 94, 95, 106, 115, 116, 117, 119
Flew, Anthony, 102, 103, 118, 119
Freud, Sigmund, 33, 34, 35
Freudian critique of religion, 33–5

Gandhi, Mahatma, 67, 68, 101
Ganges, 81
Genesis, 41
God, 62, 64, 65, 67, 68, 72, 79, 80, 81, 82, 84, 87, 92, 93, 96, 100, 101, 102, 103, 104, 105, 107, 110, 114, 115, 116, 117, 118, 129, 132, 133, 134, 140, 146, 155, 156, 158, 162
as acting in history, 67, 68, 70, 71
Aquinas's proofs for, 3–4
as author of specific results, 59
as causal agent, 35
as compassionate, 53, 119
as destroyer, in Śaivism, 19–22
as dynamic, 55
experiential belief in, 16
as father figure, 34
grounds for belief in, 1–31
grounds for disbelief in, 33–43
and *karma*, 1–2, 19–20, 52: in Advaita Vedānta, 55–7; in Dvaita Vedānta, 59; in Nyāya, 52–5; in Viśiṣṭādvaita Vedānta, 57–8
knowledge of, by inference, 36–41
logical proofs for, 14, 15
and *māyā*, 56
mystical experience of, 18
ontological argument for, 7–10, 11, 13, 14
pragmatic belief in, 23–24
and problem of evil, 46–7, 49, 52: in Advaita Vedānta, 55–7; in Dvaita Vedānta, 59; in Nyāya, 52–5; in Viśiṣṭādvaita Vedānta, 57–8
as revealer of scripture, 35–6
and revelation, 13
role of, in Nyāya, 2
as supervisor of *karma*, 52–3
Udayana's proofs for, 2–3, 118
Gopīs, 71
guṇas, 63, 64
guru, 7, 34

Hare, R. M., 105, 106, 107, 115
Hari-Hara, 157
heaven, 132, 135
Hindu conception of, 134–5
Heilsgeschichtliche view, 67
hell, 132, 134, 135
demythologisation of, 135
Hindu conception of, 134–5
Herman, Arthur L., 52
Hick, John H., 18, 19, 47, 94, 100, 105, 106, 107, 111, 112, 113, 117, 129, 130, 135, 136, 140, 141, 142, 143, 144, 146, 148, 149, 152, 153, 162, 163
Hinduism, 1, 2, 3, 7, 15, 16, 20, 33, 63, 64, 67, 68, 70, 71, 74, 75, 78, 85, 92, 93, 101, 108, 112, 119, 126, 131, 134, 140, 156, 159, 161, 162
devotional, 133
doctrine of *karma* and reincarnation in, 140–9
four strands in, 158
heaven in, 132–4
hell in, 134–5
incarnation in, 72–3
and monotheism, 22
and polytheism, 22
and problem of evil, 47
and religious pluralism, 152, 154, 156
and science, 42–3
soul and identity in, 131
theistic, 72, 79, 87, 109, 131, 157, 158

Hindu linguistic theory, 85
Hindu thought, schools of, 48, 156, 157
  absolutistic, 78, 82–5
  and doctrine of rebirth, 137
  evil in, 48–9
  God and *karma* in, 53–4
  and concept of personality, 132
  and reconciliation, 157
  theistic, 78, 82–5, 87
  see also Mīmāṁsā, Nyāya, Sāṅkhya, Vaiśeṣika, Vedānta, Yoga
Hindu thought, 95, 96, 100, 112, 113, 114, 128, 160
Hiriyanna, M., 7, 8, 9, 10, 15, 24, 51, 56, 88
history, Hindu,
  classical period, 74
  Vedic period, 74
Hobbes, 92
holy spirit, 73
Humanism, 156
Hume, David, 4, 153

ideas, Platonic, 125
identity, personal, 129, 131, 142, 143, 144
  empirical, 131
  eschatological, 131
  and resurrection, 129, 130
  and the soul, 131
ignorance,
  and evil in Advaita Vedānta, 55
  and knowledge in Advaita Vedānta, 55
  origin of, in Advaita Vedānta, 55–6
image worship, 72
incarnation, 72, 73
  as beginningless regress, 145–6
Indian Independence Movement, 68
individuals and *karma*, 50, 51
Indra, 95
inequality, 48
inference, 6, 11, 12, 35, 66, 101
  deductive, 38
  inductive, 38
  materialist rejection of, 37–41
intuition, 18
  direct, 15
Islam, 154, 156, 158
Israel, 67, 155
Īśvara, 6, 7, 9, 10, 65, 104, 110
Īśvarapraṇidhāna, 110
itihāsa, 66
Itihāsas, 69, 70, 74

Jainas, 18, 32
Jainism, 18, 140
jāti, 129
Jeans, Sir James, 87
Jennings, J. C., 148
Jesus Christ, 72, 73, 81, 152, 158
Jews, 65, 155
jīvanmukti, 108, 109
jñāna, 82, 83, 84, 133
jñānakāṇḍa, 66
Joshua, 81
Judaism, 73, 91, 140, 159
  and resurrection, 128–9
Judeo-Christian tradition, 1, 22, 23, 24, 116, 131, 134
Jyotiṣṭoma rite, 33

Kabīr, 75
kaivalya, 9, 110
Kant, I., 14, 56, 124, 125, 126
karma, 1, 2, 19, 20, 22, 59, 103, 109, 119, 132, 134, 135, 144
  as beginningless, 56, 58
  collective, 149
  doctrine of, 49–50
  as ethical, 51
  as explanation for evil, 49–52
  and God, 52: in Advaita Vedānta, 55–7; in Dvaita Vedānta, 59; in Nyāya, 52–5; in Viśiṣṭādvaita Vedānta, 57–8
  and reincarnation, doctrine of, 140–9
  theory of, 141, 148
  in Viśiṣṭādvaita Vedānta, 58
knowledge, 65, 66, 79, 83, 85, 114, 115, 117

Hindu philosophical sources of, 39
and ignorance in Advaita Vedānta, 55
materialist source of, 41
parataḥ – prāmāṇya, 114
in reincarnation, 147
svataḥ prāmāṇya, 113, 114
testimony, as source of, 40
Western philosophical sources of, 39
kriyā, 133
Kṛṣṇa, 71, 72, 162
Kumarappa, 58
Kumārila, 18
Kuntī, 34
Kusumāñjali, the, 25

lakṣaṇā, 80, 81
ajahallakṣaṇā, 81
gauṇa vṛtti, 81
jahadajahallakṣaṇā, 81
jahallakṣaṇā, 81
language, 35, 36, 78, 158, 159
religious, 78–88, 91, 96, 113, 158, 162: in absolutistic school, 82–5; as cognitive, 115; cumulative meaning of, 82–5; equivocal, 80; as factual statements, 91, 100, 115, 116; as impartite, 79, 83, 85; as non-cognitive, 91, 104, 105; as non-factual statements, 120; as relational, 78; as symbolic, 79, 82; in theistic school, 82–5; and Thomistic analogy, 80–2; univocal, 80; utilitarian, 96
Lazarus, 42
Leviticus, 70
līlā, 56, 57
living liberation, 108, 109, 110
Livy, 92
logical critique of God, in Materialism, 38
Logical Positivism, 37, 94, 96, 97, 106, 116, 117, 118, 119, 120, 147
and materialist critique of God's existence, 41
Lokāyata, school of, 32; *see also* Cārvākas, Materialism
Lotz, H., 14
Luther, Martin, 33

Madhva, 11, 18, 59; *see also* Dvaita Vedānta
Mahābhārata, the, 70, 71
Mahārāṣṭra saints, 75
Maharṣi, Ramaṇa, 20
Mahāvīra, 18
manas, 125, 126
Manusmṛti, 70, 74
Marx, Karl, 33
Marxism,
in India, 33
Marxist critique of religion, 32–3
Materialism, 4, 5, 22, 24, 32, 33, 126, 127
and logical critique of God, 35–41; *see also* Cārvākas
māyā, 56, 57, 104
and Īśvara, 56–7
and perception, 56
memory, 128
in reincarnation, 142, 144, 145
Mīmāṁsā, *see* Pūrva Mīmāṁsā
Mīmāṁsaka(s), 64, 65, 87
mind, 126, 127, 130, 144
as simple entity, 124, 125
as complex unity, 124, 125
miracles, 16, 17, 153
Hindu attitude towards, 17, 42
Miśra, Vācaspati, 53, 128
Mitchell, Basil, 106
mokṣa, 93, 97, 99, 133, 145, 162
monism, 64, 87, 134
qualified, *see* Viśiṣṭādvaita Vedānta
monist Hindus, 155
Monotheism,
Hindu, 22, 158
Judeo-Christian, 22, 23
Western, 22
Moody, R. A. Jr., 135
morality, 22, 93
and *karma*, 19–20, 149

moral argument for God's existence, 19, 20
moral reasoning, 97
Muḥammad, 140
Murty, K. Satchidananda, 42, 81, 87
Muslims, 93
mystical experience, 18, 162
Hindu conception of, 163
mysticism, unitive, 162
myth, 71, 73, 153

Nāgeśa, 109
Nālāyira-Prabandham, 74, 75
nāma, 86
Nammālvār, 74, 157
nature, 4, 5, 156
and the teleological argument, 5, 32
Neo-Hinduism, 154
New Testament, 17, 58, 65
Nirvāṇa, 156, 162
nitya, 69
Niyoga, 33
non-dualism, 131, 133, 158; *see also* Advaita Vedānta, monism
noumenon, 162
Nyāya, school of, 1, 2, 5, 6, 11, 52, 53, 55, 57, 58, 92, 114, 115, 119
epistemological categories of, 101
God and *karma* in, 52–5
līlā in, 57
origin of Vedas in, 65
and teleological argument, 5–6
Nyāyakusumāñjali, 2, 24
Nyāyasūtra, 2
Nyāya-Vaiśeṣika, school of, 3, 115, 124, 125
concept of soul in, 125–6
concept of universals in, 125, 129

Old Testament, 65
ontological argument, 7–10, 11, 13, 14

pain, 47
absence of, 125
as associated with pleasure, 51
Pantheism, 156
parārtha, 40
Pantañjali, 7, 23, 24, 110
perception, 12, 37, 66, 101, 114, 163
external, 39, 40
internal, 39, 40
of God direct, 15
and *māyā*, in Advaita Vedānta, 56
personality, 137, 143
Hindu concept of, 132
Western concept of, 132
phenomena, 162
philosophy of analysis, 116
philosophy of religion, 88, 92, 104, 113, 116, 117, 118, 141, 153
Western, 37, 78, 79, 99, 113, 114, 163
Plato, 124, 125, 126, 129, 131
Platonic ideas, 125
pleasure,
as associated with pain, 51
polymorphism, 22
polynominalism, 22
Polytheism, 39
Hindu, 22, 95, 158
Positivism; *see* Logical Positivism
Potter, Karl H., 97, 98, 99, 147
Pradyumma-Īśvara, 157
prakṛti, 5, 6, 9, 10, 64
prakṛtilayas, 10
pramāṇa, 37, 115
praṇava, 7
prasthānabheda, 157
pratyakṣa, 101; *see also* perception
Premchand, 102, 103
proofs, of God's existence, 118
Aquinas, 3–4
Hindu, 23–5
Udayana, 2–3
Yoga, 6–10
psychoanalysis, 146, 147
Purāṇas, 66, 69, 70, 71, 74
puruṣa(s), 5, 6, 7, 9, 10, 109

quality, 125

Quantum theory, 87, 148

Radhakrishnan, S., 15, 54, 135, 154
rājasī, 63, 109
Rāma, 70, 72
Rāmanāma, 68
Rāmānuja, 11, 12, 13, 15, 57, 58, 59, 74, 75, 83, 84, 87, 88, 158
  critique of cosmological argument, 13; of ontological, 13; of teleological, 11–12
Rāmāyaṇa, 70, 75
realization,
  God, 53, 66
  self, 97, 158
reason, 11, 14, 15, 93
rebirth, 141
  animal, 135
  doctrine of, 49, 50, 137
reincarnation, 130, 145, 146
  and *karma*, doctrine of, 140–9
religion,
  and culture, 159, 160
  as human phenomenon, 159, 161
  non-theistic, 162
religious pluralism, 152, 162
  in India, 152
  philosophical significance of, 153–4
  Western approaches to, 155, 159, 162
religious reality, 96, 97, 101, 115, 158, 160, 161, 162
  impersonal, 162
resurrection, 128–32, 140; *see also* survival, post mortem
resuscitation,
  and near death experiences, 135–8
revelation, 11, 13, 15, 18–19, 42, 62, 63, 64, 65, 66, 74, 75, 82, 92, 93, 161
Ṛg Veda, 63, 74
ritual, 65, 66, 153
Roman Catholic church, 73
Roy, Rammohun, 17, 42
ṛṣis, 69, 71

śabda – pramāṇa, 39, 70
śabda-tattva, 86
saccidānanda, 84
sādhanā, 133
Śaiva saints, 75
Śaiva Siddhāntin, 21
Śaiva theism, 19, 20
Śaivism, and sectarian reconciliation, 157–8
Śaiva arguments for God's existence, 20
sālokya, 133, 134
salvation, 22, 23, 107, 111, 125, 129, 132, 134
samādhi, 110
sāmānādhi – karaṇya, 79
sāmānya, 125
Sāma Veda, 74
sāmīpya, 133, 134
saṁsāra, 7, 56, 112, 147
saṁsarga, 78
saṁskāras, 63
saṁvādipravṛtti, 114
samvedana, 147
Śaṅkara, 42, 55, 58, 82, 83, 84; *see also* Advaita Vedānta
Sāṅkhya, school of, 5, 22, 23, 107, 109, 110, 151, 161
  and *dukkha*, 47
Sāṅkhya-Yoga, school of, 9, 108, 158
Sanskritic-Brahmanical culture, 74
Santayana, G., 101
śarīras, 144
  gross, 144
  subtle, 144
  causal, 144
sārṣṭi, 133, 134
sārūpya, 133, 134
Sarvadarśanasaṅgraha, 32, 39
śāstra, 63
sat, 84, 133
satori, 162
sattā, 125
sattva, 63
sāttvikī, 63
satya, 82, 83, 84

Sautrāmaṇi sacrifice, 34
sāyujya, 133, 134
science, 116, 160
  and factual statements, 95
  and Hinduism, 42–3
  Western, 41, 148
scientific verification, 98
scripture, 13, 32, 64, 82, 93
  authority of, 13–15, 92, 145, 147
  as beginningless, 35–6
self, the, 72, 142
Seshagiri, Rao, K. L., 63
Śiva, 19, 20, 21, 22, 132, 157, 158
  as destroyer of the universe, 20, 21, 22
śloka, 74
Smart, Ninian, 20
Smith, W. C., xvi, 59, 160, 161
smṛti, 68–76
  and non-propositional view of revelation, 69, 70
soul, 32, 124, 125, 126, 127, 133, 135
  dependence on Brahman in Viśiṣṭādvaita Vedānta, 57–8
  Hindu reincarnation of, 140
  and identity, 131
  immortality of, 124, 129
  Platonic idea of, 124–5, 129, 131
soul-body relationship, 126
  Hebraic concept of, 126–7
  materialist concept of, 126–7
  spiritual concept of, 126
sphoṭa(s), 85, 86
śraddhā, 33, 63, 64
Srinivasachari, P. N., 15
śruti, 68–76
  and propositional view of revelation, 68, 70, 75
Stoics, 155
subjectivity, 19
substance, 125
  simple, 124
  composite, 124
suffering, 47, 48, 49, 53, 103
  Hindu concept of, 48
  Western concept of, 48
Śūnyatā, 162
sūtras, 74
svabhāva, 5
svabhāvavāda, 4
svārtha, 52
svarūpa, 79
svataḥ – prāmāṇya, 114
Śvetaketu, 34, 35

Tagore, R., 75, 101
Taittirīya Upaniṣad, 78, 82
tāmasī, 63, 109
Tamilnadu, 74
Tantrism, 74
Tao, the, 162
Teleological argument, 3–4, 38
  materialist critique of, 4
  and nature, 5
  and Nyāya, 5
  Rāmānuja's critique of, 11–12
  Sāṅkhya critique of, 5
testimony, 92
  as source of knowledge, 40
Tevāram, the, 75
Theism, 16, 18, 22, 23, 33, 41, 91, 100, 112, 116, 119, 156
  Hindu, 19, 20, 79, 108, 111, 112, 117, 131, 134
  Judeo-Christian, 107, 112
  and living liberation, 110
  Saivist, 20
theistic,
  devotion, 117
  morality, 127
  schools in Hinduism, 78: and language, 82–5
theists, 64, 101, 102, 113
Theravāda Buddhism, 149
Tiruvācakam, the, 75
Tiruvāymoḷi, 74, 75
trimūrti, 21
truth, 62, 64, 65, 79, 93, 94, 95, 96, 97, 98, 100, 104, 106, 115, 116, 117, 119, 156
  eternal, 124
  in Hinduism, 154, 159
  as relative, 161
  and truth-claims, 161–2
truth claims, religious, 153
  approaches to, 155, 159, 162
  conflicting, 153, 155, 156, 159

Hindu response to, 154, 156
historical treatment of, 159–62
and truth, 161–2
Tulasi Dās, 75

ubhayavedānta, 74, 75
Udayana, 2, 3, 4, 15, 24, 25, 118
compared with Aquinas, 4
proofs for God's existence, 2–3
universals, 124, 125, 129
Nyāya-Vaiśeṣika concept of, 124–5, 129
Platonic concept of, 124
Unseen power, *see* Adṛṣṭa
upādhi, 127
upamāna, 39, 101
Upaniṣads, 66, 73, 74, 75, 78, 79, 82, 83, 84, 88
Uttaramīmāṁsā, 65, 66

Vaiṣṇavas, 75
Vaiṣṇavism, 177
and sectarian reconciliation, 157–8
Vākyapadīya, the, 86
vāsanās, 148
Vedānta, school of, 1, 13, 42, 55, 64, 66, 74, 75, 80, 87, 114, 115, 141, 162
doctrine of *karma* and rebirth in, 144–8
schools of, 52
Vedāntadeśika, 158
Vedāntasūtras, 54, 75
Vedāntins, 65, 66
Vedas, the, 3, 6, 13, 15, 32, 33, 35, 36, 59, 63, 65, 66, 69, 70, 74, 76, 80, 85, 88, 92, 116, 145, 161
authority of, 93: in Pūrva Mīmāṁsā, 66; in Vedānta, 66
as eternal, 87
origin of: in Advaita Vedānta, 64; in Mīmāṁsā, 64; in Nyāya, 65
verifiability, 99, 104
of religious statements, 94, 95, 96
verifiable claims, 91, 92
verification, 98, 99, 101, 108, 111, 113, 114, 115
verification principle, 94, 97, 100, 104
vidvān, 109
vidyā, 74
Vidyāraṇya, 83
Vijñānabhikṣu, 157
Viśiṣṭādvaita Vedānta, 52, 59, 75
Brahman's perfection in, 58
God and *karma* in, 57–9
soul's dependence on Brahman in, 57–8
Viśiṣṭādvaitin, 79
Viṣṇu, 59, 74, 132, 157, 158
vivarta, 86
Vivekacūḍāmaṇi, 49
vi-yoga, 9
vyāpti, 38; *see also* concomitance
Vyāsa, R., 10, 59, 109, 147
vyūha, 72

Weber, Max, 102
Western,
concept of moral values, 20
philosophy, 37, 156
philosophy of religion, 37, 78, 79, 99, 113, 114; absence of doctrine of *karma* and reincarnation in 141–2; concept of personality, 132; sources of knowledge, 39
Wisdom, John, 100, 102
Woods, James Haughton, 147
works, 63, 133
worldview, Hindu, 43, 99

yadṛcchāvāda, 105
Yahweh, 162
Yajur Veda, 74
Yam(a) Yamī Sūkta, 33
yoga, 133
Yoga, school of, 1, 6, 7, 9, 10, 11, 23, 109, 110, 111, 157
and proofs for God's existence, 6–10
Yogasūtras, 7, 109, 110, 147
yogī, 42, 145, 147

Zimmer, Heinrich, 132, 135, 152